World Society

World Society

JOHN W. BURTON

University College London

CAMBRIDGE

At the University Press 1972

Published by the Syndics of the Cambridge University Press
Bentley House, 200 Euston Road, London NW1 2DB
American Branch: 32 East 57th Street, New York, N.Y.10022

Library of Congress Catalogue Card Number: 71–176252

ISBNs: 0 521 08425 3 hard covers
ISBNs: 0 521 09694 4 paperback

Printed in Great Britain
by C. Tinling & Co. Ltd, London and Prescot

Contents

Acknowledgements

The author and publisher are grateful to the following for granting permission to use copyright material: to the Institut National de la Statistique et des Etudes Economiques for figs. 1, 2 and 3 (from *Tableaux de l'économie française* (1956); to The Clarendon Press for fig. 5 (from the *Oxford Economic Atlas of the World,* 3rd edition, 1965); to Penguin Books for figs. 6, 7, 8 and 9 (from Brian M. Foss (ed.) *New Horizons in Psychology,* 1966); to the *British Journal of Psychology* for fig. 10 (from L. S. and R. Penrose, *British Journal of Psychology,* 49 (1958), 31; to the University of London Press Limited for fig. 11 (from James M. Thyne, *The Psychology of Learning and Techniques of Teaching,* 1963); and to the Hutchinson Publishing Group Limited for figs. 12, 13 and 14 (from M. L. Johnson Abercrombie, *The Anatomy of Judgment,* 1960).

Preface

This study of world society is designed principally for the student at college or university, but also for those generally who want to know about recent thinking among scholars. The studies of man, that is the social and political sciences, are becoming as difficult to understand as have been the natural sciences. This is because scientific studies move from observation and description to analysis and theories. In behavioural studies as in physics, there is first observation and then theories about the behaviour of the systems being observed. At this latter stage, which the social and political sciences have now reached, the scientists concerned use a language that is unfamiliar to others. Happily, however, as scholars become clearer in their own minds they are able to express themselves in simpler language. In the course of time laymen become familiar with many scientific terms and techniques. There is thus a meeting point at which it is possible to establish communication between the two. The basic essentials and jargon of space travel are understood today by large numbers of people. So, too, with 'International Relations' – the study of world society. A decade or so ago it was generally intelligible because it was, in essence, descriptive diplomatic history: it was concerned with government policies, diplomatic happenings, and the lives of diplomats and statesmen. In the last few decades it has become analytical. Models, mathematics and a special language have made this subject, which is of vital concern to everyone, the special preserve of a few. There are not many people who can read and follow the majority of books now being published about world society, and how it functions. There must always be some special preserves, skilled techniques and a professional language, because this is the way advances in knowledge are made. But the essentials of recent thinking about world society are now becoming clearer. Its application to actual situations and to policies is beginning to seem sensible. At the same time everyone is more familiar than ever before with world affairs and with some of the terminology and models used in the study of world society, especially those drawn from other studies. There is now much that scholar and citizen can share.

Recent experience in teaching International Relations to first year undergraduates gives reason to believe that an analytical, inter-disciplinary approach to behaviour in world society is well within the comprehension of school-leavers. Indeed, they appear to be more interested and involved in their studies than similar students who are presented with the more usual descriptive and historically-oriented courses. It seems to be a mistake to use inadequate and unrealistic approaches to a subject just to make it more simple. Young people want reality and relevance. Moreover, they are not content to learn just what was taught to a generation that appears to have had no effective answers to the serious world problems of underprivilege, under-development, revolt, communal conflict and war. If it is neces-sary to introduce analytical models and unfamiliar terms, then this is acceptable to them provided there is some perceived movement towards more realistic and rewarding studies of world society.

In many cases our oversimplifications have been due to our own unwillingness, as teachers, to keep up with the times. Young people today accept space travel and electronic systems as part of their environment. They expect to be taught within this scientific environ-ment. For example, they see the relevance of self-guiding systems to an understanding of decision-making. Oversimplifications are some-times due to our unwillingness to adopt new concepts and to use models that are more useful than the ones with which we were taught.

The time has arrived at which world society should find a place within a secondary school syllabus. Teaching any subject outside the perspective of the whole is difficult, and it is world society that is the setting of all aspects of human behaviour. Furthermore, social awareness in a person needs to be promoted at the secondary level if it is to develop later. Young people have a strong urge towards protest and immediate, clear-cut solutions to social problems. An important part of social awareness is an appreciation of the nature of social problems. Solutions are discovered by research and thought. Protest has an important political function; but protest in the absence of considered solutions can have no effective direction. The search for solutions reveals complexity and can be disappointing and frustrating, but can be more rewarding than ineffective demonstration. Solutions, once found, usually require a consensual support before they can be incorporated in policy. At this point demonstration and publicity may be relevant because decision-makers include the mass of people in addition to political leaders; but advocacy is probably more effective. The energies of young people can be diverted towards both problem-solving and advocacy, even though the implication of each is that there are no easy answers or quick remedies.

References have been kept to a minimum; but those that have been made are to books teachers will find useful in filling out some of the themes discussed. They are books that could well be in any school or home library. To teachers I would say, if you are prepared to explore the thinking of those to whose publications I have referred, then your own excitement will be communicated to young people, and they will in turn respond with enthusiasm. They want to know about world society, its problems and their possible solutions, and what it holds in store for them.

August 1971   J.W.B.

PART ONE

Introduction

1.   *Why study world society?*

Why study world society? Why at schools and at universities are courses given to students who may not be employed in a foreign office or an international institution, and who may not teach, or research in, the subject? What is the educational or social value of a study of world society?

(i) Social responsibilities
An obvious reason is that we are all citizens of the world in addition to being citizens of our immediate society. We have opportunities to elect governments that make decisions involving war and peace, economic development, human rights, our own welfare and our relationships with other peoples. We do not want these matters, which are of increasing importance, to be outside our competence. Usually foreign policy does not figure prominently at elections, and it seems to have been widely accepted that delicate matters of security and diplomacy are best left to governments and their advisers. This may be changing: many people think that foreign policies are too important for us all not to have a knowledgeable interest in them. Solutions to major problems will be found, and policies based on these solutions will be followed, only when there is a general understanding of and consensus respecting the main issues. The study of world society needs to be built into educational systems, just as is mathematics, language, health and road safety. Only then will people be able to assert their estimates of how much should be spent on defence and how much on education and health, and in this way check the judgements of political leaders.

The press, television, scholars who write books, teachers who teach history and people generally create the political climate in which formal decisions are taken. But even when advisers and others have arrived at a solution to a problem, there is still a need for consensual support. Fluoridization of drinking water could be regarded as a

3

solution to some dental problems; but there still must be agreement on a policy to implement this finding. Scholars could find that some defensive strategies were self-defeating; but there still would have to be a widespread consensus in favour of some radical change. Prejudice, fear and tradition are as powerful in influencing the way people think as are vested interests. Some vested interests can be eliminated by revolution and structural change; but prejudice, fear and tradition are removed only by educational processes that are slow to show results.

(ii) Response to the environment
There is a more intimate reason for studying world society. Each of us at some stage lives and works in communities and organizations through which we seek security, harmonious social relationships, freedoms of many kinds and self-fulfilment generally. For this to be possible, we, as members, need to understand and to be able to influence the internal processes of our particular community or organization. But this by itself does not guarantee success. Every individual, every group – small or large – every organization or institution exists within a wider environment. It must be able to control this environment, or be able to adjust to it, and to changes in it. This interaction between a system (this is useful shorthand for 'individual, group or organization') and its environment is ignored all too often. Businesses sometimes fail, not necessarily because they are inefficient internally, but because there have been false predictions about changes in foreign markets, about technological developments, or about future political conditions. States find themselves involved in war, not necessarily because of an aggressive intent, but merely because they misjudged or were unaware of the longer-term responses of others to their policies.

The study of world society is the study of the total environment in which the behaviour of individuals, groups, nations and states occurs. The social and political behaviour of others is the social and political environment of each system. The behaviour of one part of a society affects the behaviour of others. This is increasingly the case in contemporary conditions of communications. The values, expectations, sympathies and hostilities of people in one place are transmitted throughout the whole of societies, and world society. Movements of independence and social reform, and even writings about these topics in any one country, affect behaviour in others. Furthermore, increased interdependence, which is the consequence of increased specialization, industrialization and trade, leads to change everywhere when there is change anywhere. Whatever our occupation or interests, each of us needs to be informed about our wider environment, how we affect it, and how we are affected by it. In particular, we need to have insights into changes that are likely to occur, such as population growth, technological change, social and political change and market changes, so that we can anticipate them, and plan our individual and collective lives accordingly.

(iii) Patterns of behaviour

A related reason is that by studying world society we are able to discover patterns of human behaviour, a knowledge of which helps us to understand and influence conditions of immediate concern to us. When societies are suddenly confronted with unrest and riots, there is a strong tendency to attribute them to a few mischief-makers, to some foreign ideology, to some particular grievance, or to conflict involving religion or race. This may be an accurate diagnosis. But if those studying world society see patterns of unrest, at universities, between communities, in industry and within states, in which there is a common variable, such as absence of a sense of participation in decision-making, then there is good reason to re-examine the local disturbance. Perhaps there has been a wrong diagnosis, and an unhelpful remedy. There are many domestic problems that are more readily understood by examining the same kind of problem on the larger scale of relationships in world society. The failure at the inter-state level of judicial processes whenever important political issues are at stake helps us to understand similar failure at the industrial level. Failure of threats such as were made by the United States of America in Vietnam helps us to understand better the limitations of deterrent strategies in dealing with communal conflict such as has occurred in Northern Ireland. There are patterns of human behaviour that occur at many levels of human organization, and because they are more conspicuous at the level of world society it is sometimes useful to observe them there.[1]

(iv) A matter of perspective

We now realize that it is important in studying and influencing human relations to adopt the widest possible perspective. The social worker does not confine his attention to Jim who is in trouble; he wants to look at Jim in the total perspective of family and school relationships. The medical general practitioner prefers to have the whole family on his list for the same reason. The town planner knows it is not sufficient merely to ensure that each house is built well, for relationships of houses with the rest of the social environment are important. Studying national history, and viewing the world from the point of view of one nation, leads to prejudice and distorted images of other peoples. The most reliable starting point in learning is usually with the whole, leaving parts to be examined in the perspective of the whole. History and geography are best taught by first making a broad survey, and later filling in the details. We learn to find our way about a town by looking at a map of the whole, and finding where we are in relation to the whole. We find our way in and out of complex buildings by having an image or a map of the whole, and our present position in relation to it – or follow notices provided by someone who has such an image. A knowledge of world society as a whole helps us to understand parts of it, and to see relationships between the parts. Without this knowledge we are likely to misinterpret behaviour, to attribute wrong motivations, to mistake individual differences for racial or cultural differences, and generally to be inadequate within our own social relationships.

(v) The study of norms
Another reason for studying world society is to determine norms of behaviour on a universal basis, and in this way to clarify many problems of less extensive social relationships.

Norms of behaviour and the nature of an ethical system are topics of interest in relation to all social behaviour. Even now there has been discovered no clear demarcation between mores that are ethical, and those that are cultural, religious, legal or merely a matter of etiquette. This failure to distinguish ethics from culturally based normative rules leads to the making of moral judgements by some sections of a community on the behaviour of others, and to the imposition of rules that have no basis other than tradition, religion, class or ethnic conventions and laws formulated to cater for special interests. Social tensions and conflicts must result. This same failure to distinguish ethics from cultural norms is even more serious in its consequences when culturally based rules are asserted in world society. The only morality or ethical system that is applicable in world society is that which arises out of the whole. It may be that, just as parts can better be understood in relation to wholes, so a better perspective can be obtained of morality within limited social relationships by looking at it in the perspective of universal norms.

Political behaviour is that behaviour which to the unit concerned is the most relevant and the most beneficial in the environmental circumstances as perceived by it, and in the light of its values and expectations. The study of the political behaviour of a unit is the study of response to its political environment. It is also the study of the ways in which a unit modifies its political behaviour as a result of responding to the environment, for response is an educational process, one of continuing interaction between the unit and its environment. What is right, that is, the most appropriate response as judged by it, cannot be assessed by what is right for others. The purpose of political analysis is to describe and to explain perceptions and responses, and to predict outcomes, but not to make valuations of response on any normative or moral basis. Probabilities of behaviour, based on observations of the behaviour of other political units in similar circumstances provide some limited possibilities of generalization, but 'norms' used in this probabilistic sense do not necessarily have any connection with 'norms' used in the moral or legal sense. In this respect political behaviour is no different from economic behaviour. There are universal laws of supply and demand based on individual response to economic options, and economists study these. These are market, but not normative rules. So, too, in political theory; it is political response to the environment that is the subject of study, and there are probably behavioural rules governing this. It is these rules that political science seeks to determine.

The political attitudes persons have to each other, especially persons of different cultural background, reflect their belief that the political behaviour of others is due to their special and even unique features, and not to patterned response to the environment. 'Original sin', and degrees of 'ability' and 'intelligence' associated with different ethnic, religious and other groups are widely held responsible for the political behaviour of persons, groups and nations. This is most clearly demonstrated when groups are in conflict, and each has the same mirror image of the other: unreliable, dishonest, aggressive, emotional, irrational and morally inferior. After conflict and the establishment of peaceful relations these features apparently undergo a change: the Japanese, before and during the war were seen to be crafty, sly and mere imitators; but are now seen to be intelligent, restrained and trustworthy traders. History is written in terms that indicate the prejudices and notions the writer has regarding leaders and peoples of other cultures. Generalizations abound in conventional wisdom about the behaviour of Germans, Chinese, Japanese, Jews and others, even though in each case the generalizations are arrived at as a result of observations made of behaviour in a few cases and in special environmental circumstances, and cannot logically be applied generally to any whole ethnic group. Political attitudes are typically culturally bound. Comparative politics tend to be based on norms of one culture, and not on norms that are universal. There is in the practice of politics, and in most theory, little recognition of the essential nature of politics, namely, the way in which, universally, political units allocate their resources within the context of their perceived environment.

Normative attitudes so much influence relations between political units, especially relations between states, that it is of interest to speculate why this is so. In so doing, some clarification of the concept of morality may occur. The biological habit of experiencing parts and progressively building up wholes is probably important in an explanation of both religious belief and normative approaches to behaviour. The environment that is outside our own experience is not explicable in terms of our experience. We are aware of it and therefore endeavour to explain it to ourselves somehow or other. The weather, on which people have depended so much for their livelihood, could be explained at one stage only by reference to supernatural forces. Social myth and prejudice have a similar origin: they help to explain observed differences in cultures and traditions not otherwise understood. They provide a framework into which unknowns can be fitted. Related to this are normative approaches to behaviour. Judgements of what is moral, conforming, ethical and good, probably rest upon comparisons between experience within the immediate social group and observations made of the behaviour of others. Barbarians and infidels were those who had different values, cultural habits and religious beliefs. The reference international lawyers make to practices of 'civilized societies' is of the same type: cultures that do not observe our rules are uncivilized. The proposition that all behaviour is a response to the environment in ways best calculated to achieve given purposes in the light of knowledge available, and that, therefore, it is of equal quality, is not one that can be accommodated within a religious or normative framework. Yet it is one that would be advanced if the observer were to commence with the whole of world society, and to observe the similarities in patterns of political behaviour as economists observe patterns that are universal.

'Morality' associated with normative standards and religious beliefs is of a low ethical order. It is behaviour expected by us of others as though they were required to respond to their environmental circumstances (including our behaviour) in the ways in which we respond to our environment. It is an insular morality we impose on others. It is morality arising in one society and claimed to be applicable universally. Even in this one it has little ethical quality. This is clear in cases in which our behaviour induces a response that we regard as immoral. An example was the response of Germany and Japan to conditions imposed by the environment – by other states – during the Great Depression. The inconsistencies of normative morality are obvious even in legal instruments, such as the United Nations Charter, which makes arbitrary distinctions between aggression and defence. Legal notions of human rights that lead to criticism of the detention of political opponents but support 'just' wars which are costly in terms of denial of a right to live, provide another example. The only normative approach that can have a moral quality is one that reflects basic and universal patterns of response to the environment. The use of violence in the defence of a position of privilege cannot be regarded as more 'moral' than its use in trying to eliminate privilege. What is ethical and what is not is a question that should not be asked at any behavioural level that is not universal. The level of morality relates to the level of social behaviour. 'Morality' conceived at a small group level and applied universally will be incompatible with norms of behaviour that arise out of experience at a higher level of social organization.

These are amongst the reasons why we study world society. Some relate to means of learning, some to practical considerations of adjustment to the environment, and some to responsibilities of citizenship.

2. *The approach*

Let us now take a brief look at the history of the study of world society, and the different approaches that have been adopted.

(i) Stages in thinking
The study of world society has passed through many stages even during this century, and especially during the last two decades. Trends in thought occur in response to changes in the environment in which scholars are thinking. This environment has two interacting features. There are the changes that occur in the structure of world society due to population growth, discovery, invention, political developments, improvements in communications, education and social organization. There is also the environment of scholarship. Knowledge and techniques in one area, such as economics, psychology and engineering, provide insights and methods that are relevant to other areas, such as education and international relations. Innovation and thinking in any one field promote innovation and thinking in many others, with the result that in all disciplines the rate of discovery is an ever increasing one.

One of the consequences of this interaction has been a far greater interest in recent years in world society and behaviour of peoples within it as a subject for study. The narrower interest in institutions and relations between state authorities is waning because of greater interest in human behaviour and social organization at all levels. Furthermore, world society is itself in the process of making a choice, or altering its behaviour. It is less and less pursuing political and constitutional means of organizing its affairs and solving its problems, and more and more employing specific, universal, professional institutions to control and coordinate activities. State and local government authorities will continue to make available many kinds of services, such as local law and order, and the facilities for culture, education and health. Universal institutions, some coordinating the views and activities of governments, some that are private, are more and more taking over regulation of common services, such as civil aviation, communications, the coordination of standards in health, scientific exchanges, and many other activities of universal concern.

This interaction between the environment of the real world and the environment of scholarship can be seen in the successive stages of rapid growth in the study of world society. Each of these stages can be distinguished and described, even though each has led into the next in a continuous stream of thought. (Social scientists have a habit of breaking down continuing events or trends into separate parts or steps just to examine them in detail: their continuity should, nevertheless, be kept in mind.) They are similar to the steps that have been taken in the development of other behavioural studies. To commence with there are broad generalizations based on some primitive notions of human behaviour, then more precise descriptions of particular features, and, in due course, the application of scientific methods, including, where possible, controlled observations and quantification.

Philosophy: Even before the modern world society emerged, thinkers were interested in relations between states, the origins of war, the conditions in which wars were 'just', how to achieve the aims of governments, how best to exercise power and other questions of this nature. Some believed that problems of peace and war related to the nature of man, others to the interference of governments in the commercial and other dealings of citizens, and still others to the existence of states and the absence of any central authority. The works of Dante in the fourteenth century, Thomas More and Machiavelli in the sixteenth century, Grotius in the seventeenth century, William Penn at the turn of the century, Rousseau, Kant, Bentham in the eighteenth century, James Mill and the Quakers of the nineteenth century, fall into these categories.[2]

Institutions: Practical men of affairs were quickly persuaded that inter-governmental institutions were necessary if wars were to be prevented, and if peaceful transactions were to be promoted. The settlements of Westphalia in the seventeenth century and Vienna in the nineteenth century were evidence of this. The First World War gave added weight to the argument that an international collective security institution was required. National defences, alliances and power balancing systems seemed to have failed. The thinking of scholars reflected these practical considerations, and at the end of the last century and the beginning of this one attention was given, not so much to the causes of war, but to institutional ways of preventing it. There is still a great interest in institutions as is in evidence in the works of many scholars who have written about the League and the United Nations, and possible alterations to the latter.

Law: Clearly lawyers would be interested in international problems, and in endeavours to apply to the international society the rules and procedures that had evolved in maintaining law and order within states. Attempts have been made to determine the differences between domestic and international society, and to develop codes of behaviour governing diplomatic relations, trade, war and other inter-state transactions. Lawyers have been specially interested in international institutions as providing the beginnings of a centralized and law-enforcing authority. There is a large number of lawyers today who are engaged in political and policy studies concerning world society.

History: Philosophers and lawyers have derived many of their beliefs about world society from their knowledge of history. Experience seemed to point to the aggressive and power-seeking nature of men and states, and to the difference in power among states, as the causes of war, and therefore to those features of world society in need of control by world institutions. But there are scholars who are straight historians. They have tried to describe, analyse and identify the main features of international society, and thus to evolve ideas about the nature of states and of the inter-state system. Perhaps there is no international affairs literature greater in size than the historical literature, though this position is now rapidly changing in favour of analytical and sociological studies.

Journalism: In more recent years there have been journalists who have taken a special interest in world affairs, and there has been widespread reporting of events, thanks to increased means of communication. Some research institutions collect and classify press reports, and treat these as important descriptive material. Some historians and students of current affairs treat them as sources of information, and journalistic interpretations are widespread. For example, events are often interpreted as being attributable to the personality of leaders, the overt pressures being exercised, and other such immediate influences which perhaps are more apparent than they are significant.

Strategic studies: An offshoot of historical and journalistic studies was a special interest in strategic studies, and associated with it, an interest in bargaining processes. Indeed, for a time in the fifties and early sixties the 'strategists' and 'bargainers' were using models that seemed to imply that an explanation of world society and a cure for its major problems could be found within a bargaining framework. For a time interest in the causes of war was once again directed into means of preventing it: the institutionalists had failed, but the 'mutual deterrent' advocates postulated another institutional means of war prevention.

Analysis: The general impression students have when they select International Relations as their study is that they will be bringing their diplomatic history up to date, concentrating on international law, learning about international institutions or studying strategic relations. They expect their teachers to be walking reference books on current affairs. There are still some scholars who adopt a descriptive approach – historical, legal, institutional or strategic. However, the general tendency, reflected in the contemporary literature, is to adopt an analytical approach, one that is more concerned, for example, with the analysis of the decision-making process than with the actual events that might have taken place in some particular country at some particular time, or more concerned with the reasons why institutions have developed the forms they now take than with the actual procedures that can be observed in particular instances. This does not mean that the study has become 'theoretical' and remote. On the contrary, this analytical approach requires a great deal of field work and detailed examination of behaviour at individual and small group levels and, so far as possible, some involvement in relations between governments, communities and groups so that they can be examined at first hand and not merely by means of documents or histories. Analytical approaches involve scholars in practical affairs for this reason.

   Some of the means adopted to obtain a closer analytical view of the subject matter show ingenious inventiveness. By 'simulation' Guetzkow[3] and others have endeavoured to examine how decisions are made. North[4] has employed 'content analysis' which is an intensive use of documents relating to a particular situation. Alger[5] has personally observed details of behaviour of participants at international institutions. Burton[6] has contrived to bring together the nominees of governments engaged in violent conflict and to observe their interactions. Singer and others[7] have gathered data and employed quantitative techniques so as to describe more accurately and to test hypotheses.

(ii) 'Behavioural science'
In the fifties these analytical studies were labelled 'behavioural science' to distinguish them from the earlier and more traditional descriptive ones. The emphasis on 'behaviour' was meant to draw attention to the interdisciplinary nature of these studies: political, psychological, economic and all other aspects were included. The use of 'science' was to assert the use of scientific method, and in particular the obtaining of data and their quantitative analysis as in other sciences. (By quantitative analysis is meant an analysis that is more reliable than the more usual intuitive one. It is an analysis that provides an objective check by comparison or measurement. Intuitively one might think that African students educated in a Western country were more friendly to it than others. A sociological type investigation of a sample group might support the opposite proposition.)

The study of world society has become interdisciplinary in several ways – that is, it has drawn from many other studies, such as economics and psychology. First, models and analogies have been borrowed from other sciences. One model that has been employed extensively has been drawn from 'cybernetics'. (Cybernetics is the study of steering, and is used in the study of decision-making to emphasize the importance of feedback from the environment and adjustment to avoid obstacles and to reach alternative goals.[8]) Second, there has been reliance upon methods of obtaining and analysing data that have been evolved in sociology and social psychology, such as public opinion surveys, sampling and others. Third, and perhaps most important, there have been attempts to apply 'General Systems Theory' and in this way to build on work already done at the level of animals, individuals and small groups for purposes of studying behaviour at the inter-state and world society levels. Clearly an individual, an animal, a plant, a social group, are all 'systems', that is, they comprise parts that are interdependent and are relevant to the one structure. All 'systems' have properties in common, and most have 'sub-systems', as for example, the electrical systems within a machine. If there are common properties then it is possible to apply findings in one system to another.[9]

The interdisciplinary character of contemporary approaches has many aspects, and is the source of serious methodological problems. The earlier philosophers were interdisciplinary in the sense that there were then no recognized specializations. A philosopher was supposed to be informed about physical laws as well as social matters. With the increasing complexity of societies, and in an endeavour, nevertheless, to be precise, specializations developed among scholars – for example, physical sciences, politics, history, law, economics, psychology, anthropology, and others. But more recently it has become clear that individual, group or other behaviour cannot be analysed and explained adequately by attention only to one aspect of it. History can record and describe, psychology and economics can explain some aspects of behaviour. It requires all disciplines to explain behaviour in such a way as to enable prediction. Furthermore, scholars have found similarities in behaviour at different levels of interaction. Much can be learned by scholars concerned with small group behaviour from scholars concerned with national or individual behaviour.

The practical problems of an interdisciplinary approach are obvious. It is impossible for one scholar to follow the literature of all studies. And group work has its own problems of communication and coordination. Various means have been adopted to overcome some of these limitations, such as the publication of abstracts or summaries of papers and books, data banks, retrieval systems; but these are at a very early stage of development, and may not turn out to provide a solution to the main problems inherent in an interdisciplinary approach. There is still no substitute for good ideas and great insights!

Trends towards quantification have been stimulated by the invention of computers, and generally by the technological and scientific revolutions of the post-war period. Inevitably they have led to what has been called a 'tool bias'. One writer reports:

> At a recent meeting of the American Sociological Association, an earnest graduate student whom I encountered at a publisher's soirée informed me that he was going to use analysis of co-variance for his dissertation. This prompted a question from me, to which he replied that he had not decided yet what he would study. Such enthusiasm for tools as opposed to products reminds one of a little boy hard at work with hammer, nails and wood, uncertain of what he is building.[10]

This tendency is likely to occur, in any event, when data are inaccessible because of secrecy, or because of the absence of resources available to seek out information by field work or direct involvement in situations. What research workers need is easy access to natural settings – despite their complexity – and not just to laboratory-type simulations.

Perhaps the greatest problem of all in a behavioural science approach to world affairs is lack of data. Most of our thinking about world society is speculative. It reflects all kinds of primitive notions about behaviour – especially the behaviour of others! Are there national and racial political traits such as aggressiveness? What are the motivations of people and nations? Is power the controlling influence in world society? Is bargaining basic in relationships? We need a lot more data before we can put to full use the mathematical and other techniques that are already available.

The reason why data are not available is not just that the subject matter of world society is complex. The main reason is that we have not devoted resources to its study. The resources used in getting a man on to the moon could have produced vast quantities of data about world society, and if there were such expenditure the problems of world society would not look quite as intractable. Unfortunately, politicians and people can comprehend space travel, cancer research, economic development and nuclear deterrence. Few are prepared to do more than shrug their shoulders at the complex problems of world society such as are presented by wars. Scholars have not yet succeeded in pointing the way sufficiently clearly to attract support for extensive research.

We have inherited our curious beliefs about behaviour in world society, and unconsciously they control our thinking. The absence of data and testing of these untested hypotheses means that they remain unchallenged. The result is that, despite attempts at being precise, quantitative or 'scientific', a good deal of scholarly work in this area remains remote or uninteresting. There is little point in understanding all about bargaining if, in reality, bargaining is not important in relationships. It could be misleading to research into international institutions with enforcement powers if, in reality, enforcement is not possible in world society. It may not be helpful to concentrate attention on supposed causes of conflict, such as poor health and inadequate education, if in reality people are seeking first and foremost independence or ethnic identification. Perhaps it is not 'scientific' research that we most need. We certainly need a scientific approach; but it must be carried out by people who have read and observed and who can pose interesting questions to be

asked and answered. Student accusations of 'irrelevance' are frequently justified.

(iii) The post-behavioural revolution

An interest in behaviour, rather than just in description, soon leads to
an enquiry into motivations and the reason why groups, governments
and institutions act as they do. Governments and institutions are
creations designed to serve the purposes of people; in the long term
they must reflect the motivations, drives, fears and ambitions of
people. Consequently, an analytical approach to world society soon
leads one to consider values held by nations and people and the ways
in which they perceive themselves, others and their environments
generally. The study becomes then a 'behavioural' one, in the literal
sense of the word. The emphasis is not just on the interdisciplinary
approach and scientific method, but on significance, relevance and
human values. It may be necessary for students of world society to
work in villages as anthropologists have done, or take time reading
creative literature by writers of countries important in this changing
world.[11]

The literature in the field of world society being published in the
present day is greatly concerned with values, authority, political
participation and social revolution.[12] Aware of these trends, and
because he was interested in the study of 'systems' and their response
to their environments, the retiring President of the American Political
Science Association in 1969 referred to the 'post-behavioural revolution' which reflected, in his view, a deep discontent with the direction
of teaching and research. He asserted that the features of this
revolution were: an insistence that substance or the field of interest
must be determined first, and methods and form introduced later; a
questioning of the traditional hypotheses on which empirical studies
are based; a closer association with the real world and its problems;
an acceptance of a responsibility to protect and to promote the
developing values of society; and active participation in world politics
so as to help promote these values. The post-behavioural revolution
did not decrease either the interdisciplinary or the scientific emphasis
of the behavioural approach. It directed more attention to human
behaviour as such, and in particular, motivations and values underlying behaviour.

Despite all its difficulties, the study of world society is now
beginning to throw some light upon the basic problems of conflict and
decision-making because it has been able to draw so much from other

areas of study. Even space exploration, and the 'feedback' mechanisms that are employed in it, has provided tools for political scientists to use. An interdisciplinary approach is a complex one, but it is less daunting than first appears because it gains from the discoveries made in the separate disciplines. Furthermore, political scientists with a sound practical, theoretical and methodological background are moving out of their libraries – and their cultures – into the wider world society, observing, and sometimes becoming involved in, the day-to-day processes of decision-making and the resolution of conflict. There is no valid objection to 'theoretical analysis' – there is nothing so practical as good theory. But to be good, that is, relevant, testable and tested, a close relationship with the subject matter being studied is essential.

A history of thought about world society shows that there has been a cumulative process – each step is built on past ones. There are not revolutions and counter-revolutions in the approach to the subject. There are additional steps as the environment changes, including discoveries in other behavioural disciplines; as the features of world society reveal themselves in events, including independence movements and campus riots; and as techniques are invented which can usefully be employed.

The intention of this study is to give students of today a means of analysing the world society of tomorrow, no matter what it turns out to be – and not just an ability to describe some contemporary event. The world society of tomorrow is likely to be far more different from the present one than is the present one from those of the past. Imagine how hard pressed states will be to preserve their passport regulations in the world of tomorrow in which far larger numbers of people will be travelling; to preserve their ideologies in the world of tomorrow in which most people will have knowledge of others by radio, television and direct contact; and to preserve forms of authority, social institutions, and values that are more and more being rejected in the new environment created by communications and new technologies. There is now a world society to be described, analysed and understood. Then, hopefully, it can be modified and regulated to meet the needs and aspirations of the human race.

3. *The scope of the study*

It will be seen that the history of thought about world society includes a steady movement away from relations between states to broader considerations. Diplomatic history is a narrower study than a study of values and motivations, though one leads to the other.

(i) 'International Relations' or 'world society'
It is because of the past preoccupation with relations between nations that 'International Relations' is the title that is usually given to the discipline concerned with the study of world politics and world society. It is an unfortunate title for our present purposes. States sometimes comprise different national groups, such as English, Irish, Scots and Welsh in the state of the United Kingdom. If we were concerned only with relations among the 150 or so independent political units of today, 'inter-state' would be a more appropriate term than 'inter-national' relations. The general idea that most of us have of world society is one that is based on maps of the world which emphasize state boundaries, on historical studies which concentrate on relations among governments. We are familiar with a set of national symbols, customs and institutions that make us feel different from peoples in other states. For this reason we think about world affairs as though they were confined to relations between states. But the study of world society is not confined to relations among states or state authorities. There are important religious, language, scientific, commercial and other relationships in addition to a variety of formal, non-governmental institutions that are world-wide.

This is not just a matter of choosing between different words. We are choosing an approach when we choose to speak of world society and not inter-national relations. The study of world society is a much wider study than the relations of units within it. It is, of course, possible and useful to study inter-state trading relations and inter-governmental institutions of various kinds. It is also possible and

19

useful to make comparative studies of the ways in which different governments behave and how their different institutions function. But these studies based on states cannot give us that understanding we seek of world society, and in particular its processes and trends. Obviously, any separation of domestic politics and world politics is arbitrary and probably misleading. For example, these state studies cannot tell us much about the nature of conflict among communities that originates within states and spills over into world society. The political and social life of people within states, which is always altering with changed thinking and new technologies, influences relations among states. This is clear where there are sudden and fundamental changes such as have taken place this century in Russia and in China. Less dramatic internal political and social changes are altering relations among states year by year. Indeed, it is because this is so that the more powerful states such as the United States of America and the Union of Soviet Socialist Republics endeavour to influence these changes in other states.

State boundaries are significant, but they are just one type of boundary which affects the behaviour of world society. There are local municipal boundaries such as those of the Greater London Council, which include more people than do many states, and in which administrative functions are carried out such as those that occur within small states. At the other end of the scale there are boundaries that include several states, such as those of the European Common Market and the Organization of African Unity. There are also non-geographical boundaries to be taken into account. These are based on functions, for example, the boundaries that separate the work of the World Health Organization from the Food and Agricultural Organization. These cut across geographical or state boundaries. The world geographical map depicting states cannot show these – but they exist and an image of world society is not complete without them.

If states controlled all world activities even to the limited extent that they control the activities of an inter-state institution like the World Health Organization, then one could extend the idea of inter-state relations to include all activities in world society. But there are many transactions in addition to those initiated and regulated by governments within states that cut across state boundaries. Indeed, new ideas and philosophies cut across state boundaries sometimes despite attempts by governments to prevent this happening. There is now one world of science. No state can afford to cut itself off from scientific and technological developments. It is not possible to import just a selection of scientific thoughts. From our own studies we know how knowledge in one subject relates to knowledge in another. Natural science and political thought cannot be separated because the one employs the methodologies and thinking of the other, and developments in the one field lead to developments in the other. Technological inventions change political and social life wherever they occur. The working life of a factory worker in a developed socialist country is little different from the life of a factory worker in another industrialized country. Similarly, administrations and cultures tend to converge with the spread of ideas, and this will occur even more rapidly when television is as widely received as radio is now.

If we employ the term 'world society' instead of 'international relations', if we approach our study in this global way instead of the more traditional 'national' way, we will tend to have a wider focus, to ask questions that are more fundamental and important to civilization, and be able to assess better the relevance of our own national behaviour to the wider world environment.

(ii) The problem of scope

Whichever approach is adopted, the problem arises where to draw the limits of enquiry. In studying the individual, to what levels of social organization must one move in order to obtain a reasonably satisfactory interpretation of behaviour? The school, the local community, the nation? No one would say that a specialized knowledge of the structure and functions of world society would be required for an adequate explanation of individual behaviour. But many aspects of world society might be relevant, for example, fear of wars. In studying world society, to what levels of social organization does one move? The nation, the decision-making authorities, the pressure groups? No one would say that a specialized knowledge of the individual would be required for an adequate explanation of national behaviour. But many aspects of the individual may be relevant, for example, the interaction of the personalities of individuals and the leadership roles they fill.

In practice we decide which 'levels of behaviour' are relevant by moving up or down, that is, from the individual to the world society or from the world society to the individual. We focus on those levels of behaviour which are relevant to what we are studying. The use of the term 'focus' helps to point to the fact that levels of behaviour are just one consideration. The problem is not merely to include in an analysis all the levels of human behaviour that are relevant. One must include also consideration of aspects of behaviour that are not confined to any level, such as participation demands and values of all kinds, which can be observed and analysed only in studies of behaviour that cut across all levels. Our problem is one of fields of study, in the examination of which aspects of all disciplines are relevant, rather than levels. No less, however, a study of human behaviour at any level and in relation to any particular aspect is best carried out within the context of world society. A study of communal conflict needs to draw on studies of conflict at all levels, and studies of the wider environment in which it takes place.

Some scholars believe that it is desirable to confine 'International Relations' to the narrower study of diplomatic history, foreign policies of states and decision-making by them. This is a clearly defined field, and one which individuals can comprehend. There can be detailed description with a minimum of generalization. Others believe that concentration on this particular field diverts attention away from the examination of underlying explanations of what is being described. Scope comes to be a matter of personal preference. Some students prefer to study International Relations, and some world society. The two different fields of study require different methods. The first tends to be descriptive, and the second tends to be analytical and conceptual. This treatment of world society adopts the latter.

4. *Conceptualizing and models*

While we may learn best by first having a knowledge of the whole, in practice, the existence of this knowledge depends upon the experiences of others who have been able – sometimes over many generations – to build up a total picture from their knowledge of parts and the relations of parts. A map is drawn by exploration of parts. The parts come first. This is the practical means of discovery. Similarly, in exploring human behaviour we, as persons, commence with the immediate social unit, and only later do we explore the interactions within and between larger societies. We discover relationships first within the family, then the kinship group, the school, the locality, the nation, and only much later in the wider environment. It is our day-to-day habit to move from local to wider knowledge, from discovery of parts to wholes. It is the way of learning in the absence of a total picture.

There are many aspects of human behaviour which cannot be taught or learned from the perspective of the whole because no one has yet managed to explore all the parts. We are still at the stage of discovery by experience. In some cases we may never complete the exploration, especially when what we are exploring is continually changing. The study of world society is of this nature. We require to know what world society as a whole looks like, what are the universal influences that determine it and the behaviour of its parts, what the reality of world society is in the sense that we can know reality by touching and testing. A description of world society could slowly be built by trial and error and by a painstaking fitting of parts. The nature of the task of building up the whole from parts can be appreciated by imagining an immense jigsaw, covering acres, the parts of which keep changing in shape but in an interacting manner such that they form a whole at any one point of time.

(i) The intellectual problem
Furthermore, there are some intellectual difficulties in approaching

23

physical and social relationships as a whole. How many of us could draw accurately, from memory, even a coastal map of any continent, let alone the inter-relations of mountains and rivers? The world would be impossible. Social and political interactions are beyond comprehension on a world scale. Young children and most adults cannot comprehend relationships beyond their immediate physical and social ones. At best we can have a concept of the whole. We need such a concept, for clearly it is not possible to teach or to research into the nature of world society in the absence of an ability to think conceptually about the thing being studied.

Because of our habit of observing parts of wholes, and concentrating on a few aspects of a complex relationship, and because of the difficulties to be met in conceptualizing wholes, we have, over the years, arrived at a division of labour by which all of some aspects of behaviour, or all the behaviour of some species, groups or individuals, are examined together within the one designated part of the whole. The disciplines of economics, psychology, social psychology, anthropology and animal behaviour are examples of this division of labour. But this specialization has not overcome the problem. The more thought develops, and the more research work is carried out in any one area, the more it seems necessary to enter into others. The economist finds he has also to be a psychologist. But he finds increasing difficulties because the study of wholes is becoming more and more difficult as the separation of the whole of human behaviour into disciplines leads to a separate language and literature in each. One consequence of this division of labour is that it seems to place general theories of human behaviour outside the competence of everyone.

So we now have to find means by which these artificial barriers can be crossed, and we have to develop 'interdisciplinary' studies. Unfortunately, there are few scholars trained in one discipline who can accommodate to the viewpoints of another. Even within multi-discipline universities there is little cross-disciplinary discussion. As a biologist once commented: 'If we had come down from the universe gradually through the hierarchy of systems to the atoms, we would be much better off. Instead we have now to resynthesize the conceptual bonds between those parts we cut in the first place.'[13]

To some degree these barriers are being broken through by new disciplines that cut across the old boundaries. For example, studies of power, communications, decision-making, conflict and many others involve most physical and social sciences. Anyone studying conflict must make himself familiar with work done on delinquency, matrimonial conflict, industrial conflict, communal and race conflict, and class conflict. While these new disciplines are an advance on past specializations, they do not provide the means towards a general theory of behaviour, or even towards a manageable synthesis of different disciplines. The departmentalization of knowledge persists. The original divisions deal with behaviour at different levels of social organization – biology, animal studies, psychology, social psychology, anthropology, sociology, politics, international politics. These new disciplines are concerned with structure and function, and touch upon each of the old disciplines, but are themselves separate from each other. A third dimension seems to be required, that is some link that touches on both sets of division of labour. Such a link could be, for example, the study of social-biological values or other studies that have a universal connotation, and which are the stuff of which a general theory of human behaviour will be made.

This points to the condition in which we are: science has moved from the study of parts immediately observable within the environment, towards conceptualization of the whole, and towards a re-examination of the parts previously observed in this total perspective. But it has moved only some distance. Town planners now place their creations in the perspective of the wider environment. Social case workers observe the behaviour of their clients in the perspective of the wider social environment in which they are living, and see behaviour less as right and wrong, and more as that response to the environment which the person considers most relevant and beneficial in the circumstances as perceived by him. Teachers are beginning to draw the attention of their students to wholes before examining parts. Cosmonauts seeing the world as a whole from outer space are impressed with the close physical relationships that exist between countries, and seem to have a perspective different in quality from any that can be obtained by travel on the earth's surface, or even from looking at global representations of the earth. But as yet we have no means by which to arrive at explanations of behaviour that take into account all of it, and the total environment in which it takes place.

In due course day-to-day experience and observation of the immediate environment could extend to wholes. Histories could be rewritten in a global instead of a national perspective, and concepts of behaviour that are at present based on what is 'normal' could give place to behavioural concepts that are less 'morally' orientated. A different perspective would be obtained of 'aggressive' and 'irrational' behaviour, and there would be modifications in attitudes towards others of other nationalities, races and religions. This result could be obtained in the course of time once communications were such as to extend the immediate environment to encompass the whole. But this is a very long-term view – a never-ending period of time.

There is, however, a short cut, or an alternative to the gigantic task of fitting together the changing pieces of the jigsaw. We can have conceptual thinking that commences with the whole, or more correctly, with models of the whole. Our concept or model is obtained by imagination drawn from experience with the parts, from conjecture, and from history and observation of contemporary behaviour at all social levels. Then we can test its validity in the real world by seeing if parts fit in as one would predict from the models. Take once again the example of discovery of the globe. An early theory, derived from observation, was that the earth was flat. But a test showed it was not. Theories are easily come by. In science it is testing that is important. Tests only disprove. Circling the world did not prove it was round, it proved it was not flat. It could have been egg-shaped. So with human behaviour. Provided we are prepared continually to test, this short cut to knowledge is a useful one.

For these reasons the earlier one breaks from the childhood habit of exploration of parts and the observation of the immediate environment, and the earlier one considers general theories, the earlier one will be able to interpret this environment in the wider perspective of the whole. In prescriptive terms, education should be directed as far as is possible towards conceptual thinking of wholes of societies, a theme which Herbert Kelman has expounded in relation to nationalism.[14]

(ii) Models and reality
Let us now look at some of the models that have been employed in thinking about world society. Before doing so, we should be clear what a model is.

The student learning about world society tends to be confused between that which conventional wisdom and practice assume to be 'reality' – for example, balance of power and other policy orientations that reflect some image of world society based on experience at one point, and at one point of time, in world society – and the conceptual models advanced by theorists who believe that the way to approximate to reality is by conceptualization of the whole, and a re-examination of the parts to see whether they fit. The conceptualization provides a hypothesis, and experience the means of testing it. If one model explains better behaviour at various levels than another, then this conceptualization is a closer approximation to reality.

It needs to be stressed, however, that images and models of reality held by actors on the world stage are to them reality. There can be many realities, and therefore different responses to the same environment. Furthermore, the images and models held of reality contribute to the creation of reality. If state authorities have in mind one explanation of behaviour and act accordingly, and force upon others relevant responses, relationships based on that behaviour will be created; freedom of choice of behaviour of any one state is limited by the actions of all others. The assumption that states are potentially aggressive is one that leads states to adopt defensive measures, alliances and collective security. Other assumptions could lead to other behaviour. The question arises, therefore, to what extent is reality merely the logical development of our assumptions, and to what extent are our images and models merely the expression of a reality we have created? They may, in fact, be telling us little or nothing about reality in world society in the more fundamental sense that we speak of physical and biological reality.

The difference between a model and an analogy needs to be noted. A model is a simplification of reality, and draws attention to those features in which the observer is interested. There are models or maps of London showing where main streets, parks and buildings are in relation to each other, diagrams showing bus and train routes, and maps showing theatres. They enable us to get from point A to point B reliably. An analogy is not a model of reality. It is a means by which some features of it can better be understood. 'Behaviour of states is like the aggressive behaviour of individuals.' This is an analogy. There may be some relation to reality in that states include individuals and individuals may be aggressive. But this association with reality, and the aggressiveness of the individual, have both to be demonstrated: they may not be present. Until so demonstrated similarities are but analogous. The tendency is to confuse analogy with reality, to confuse, that is, the use of analogy with the use of models. The use of General Systems Theory sometimes helps in determining that which individuals, small groups, communities and states have in common. Behaviour at one level can, then, be treated as a model that depicts certain features of behaviour at another. For example, if the proposition is valid that all organic systems adapt to the environment, then certain propositions regarding the behaviour of small groups, which we can examine, may be applied to the behaviour of states.

(iii) The billiard-ball model

Over the ages there have been many models or abstractions used to bring to focus different aspects of world society. At one time, when the fortunes of a nation appeared to fluctuate for no apparent reason, this could be explained by reference to the swing of a pendulum – a simple mechanical device of which everyone was aware. Even today, when conditions responsible for change are not known precisely, we are prepared to refer to a run of unfavourable events as though there were some mysterious influences determining them. In earlier times 'fate' seemed to be a sufficient explanation of events.

It is only a few hundred years since it would have been absurd to think of a world society. There was a European society, and going back much further there were Mediterranean and Chinese societies or civilizations. We know how small feudal holdings, almost tribal areas, gradually coming together, led to the establishment of provinces and nation-states. We know of the growth of empires after exploration from Europe, the movement towards independent states, and the increasing relative power of a few main states. As a consequence, we tend to have in mind a world society comprising states, small and large, each pursuing its 'national interests'. We are aware, too, of international institutions like the United Nations and its agencies, and perhaps we entertain the hope that one day there will be some world body with powers sufficient to regulate the power of states. Some such general notion of a world society of great and small states is in the back of our minds when we read of the events that unfold day by day. We interpret events in the light of this notion. Each event seems to confirm it: Soviet intervention in Czechoslovakia, United States intervention in Latin American countries and in Vietnam, the defence of spheres of influences by both of these great powers with navies, aircraft and forces deployed well outside their territorial boundaries.

This conventional image of a world composed of nation-states which are of different size and power has been termed the 'billiard-ball' model. Each state is represented by a government and is seen as an entity – a sovereign, independent unit. What takes place within the boundaries of each is not the concern of the others – this is a matter of 'domestic jurisdiction', to use the words of the United Nations Charter. The interactions or contacts are like those of different sized billiard balls. Only the hard exteriors touch, and heavier or faster moving ones push others out of the way. The points of contact are governments: it is only governments that are interacting.

This was a model that described conditions when city-states were ruled by feudal lords, when each was independent and virtually isolated from the rest of the world, when negotiation was through leaders, when the main concern was self-defence. It is a model that depicts some of the features of the contemporary world. There are direct diplomatic contacts between governments on many major matters. This same simple model of large and small balls interacting can take into account some of the internal happenings of states that affect relations with others. A new industry in one state affects an industry in another. There are internal political processes in the affected state that might result in tarriff protection: the plight of the affected industry is referred to the chamber of manufacturers, to the local member of parliament, to the minister, to the cabinet, and the government might then consult with the government of the other country. The relationship is government to government, and this fits into the idea of world society being composed of sovereign states.

It is this image which leads us to focus our attention on diplomatic relations, on governments as the main actors in world affairs, on their relative power, and on the personal characteristics of their leaders. But with this model in mind our attention is directed away from other relationships. How important are diplomats and governments in the scheme of things? To what extent is the making of policy the free decision of governments, and to what extent do governments reflect the needs and interests of others conducting their own transactions across state boundaries?

Perhaps this general notion was a realistic one many years ago; but there have been some developments in world society, which have become apparent especially since the Second World War, that are forcing us to revise our picture. For example, there is a persistent increase in the number of states, a reduction in the size of political units, and an increase in the size of economic units and the degree of interdependence. The significance of state boundaries is altering as a consequence. There are changing values or priorities in objectives, restrictions on the freedom of action of powerful states, and accentuated racial and class conflict. With education and communication there is an assimilation of ideologies leading to greater similarities between political parties within each state, and between states. These are only some of the main trends. They are interacting and not precisely defined ones. Each one of us could make his own personal list.

On the presence of one trend there will be agreement. Communications of all kinds have become quicker and more frequent between different geographical points. A great many consequences flow from this. Exchanges are promoted between persons with common and competing interests and objectives. There is a 'one world' of science, of ideas, of trade and commerce that is only marginally affected by the barriers of mountains, seas and state boundaries. Values are shared, and objectives never previously entertained are known to be practical. The peasant worker of Asia knows that other people have a higher living standard and work their own land. Peoples who do not govern themselves know that others have revolted and won independence. Asians and Africans know that non-discrimination, equality of opportunity and human dignity are values that can be attained. Communications have brought peoples into contact, and made them aware of possibilities.

Industrial technology is another undisputed influence on world society. Political units or states are not always adequate as industrial units, and specialization has led to the production of aeroplanes and other complex manufactures being spread over many countries. The oil industry knows no state boundaries, and companies make agreements with governments of different ideological outlooks. International or transnational corporations are developing, and they are not responsible to anyone but themselves. The billiard-ball model cannot depict these developments.

Another remarkable change is in values. We now know that people hold some values even higher than material gains: independence, freedom of expression, and a sense of participation in making decisions that affect them. There are psychological and sociological explanations and these we must discuss. We know that values are influencing world society and the policies of states very greatly. Probably many of these values have always been held: the serf always wanted freedom of expression and freedom from hunger. The significant difference is that now there are opportunities to demand values. Education and communications have made people aware of what is possible, and political institutions and political organizations have helped to make demands effective. The development of the ideal of a 'welfare state' has had profound effects upon the policies of states, and therefore upon world society. Once a ruler could decide upon a foreign adventure and command the service of princes and their subjects, and raise taxes to fight wars, with few political restraints imposed upon him. In the modern welfare state defence expenditure must compete with expenditure on education and other social services, and welfare generally. Even the most wealthy states find that there are political restraints on the degree to which they can sacrifice welfare needs in order to exercise their military and economic power in other countries.

Values held in world society limit the activities of great powers in other ways. Intervention in the affairs of other governments is still widespread, especially in hidden ways; but it is becoming more difficult, and more criticized publicly, especially when the citizens of the intervening state acknowledge the right of other states, small and large, to be independent. The obligation on developed states to assist developing ones – instead of exploiting them – is widely acknowledged. Principles of non-discrimination are being written into international agreements.

One value that is actively being sought in world society is racial equality. While the main racial conflict is between Europeans and others, there are also bitter conflicts developing between Asians and Africans, and among Asians and Africans. It is difficult to separate the origins of race conflict from the origins of class conflict. They have in common discriminatory policies, inequalities of income and opportunity, and the desire for equal participation in decision-making. For our purposes it is sufficient to recognize this strong desire for self-determination of communities, large and small.

Another value, reflected in the increasing demand of peoples everywhere for the right to be educated, and once educated to be employed, has many subtle effects upon the expectations of peoples and upon relations between states. Industrialization is frequently a goal in itself, even in circumstances in which there may not be strong economic arguments in favour of it. Where problems of unemployment or under-employment are not solved, political and institutional changes occur which also affect international relations.

Another trend in world society is the development of a structure of international organizations to meet the needs states have in common. 'Functional' institutions now control or influence a large part of our inter-state relations. Closely related to this tendency towards cooperation in matters of common concern is the extension of international industrial organizations. These are profit-making concerns, and they are rendering a service which otherwise would not be available. The units are often so extensive that managers and staff act very much in the capacity of administrative officials in an international governmental functional organization. Their objective is to maintain good relations with their host government. They must conform with local law, and agreements reached result in a contribution being made by them to the local economy.

These trends are creating a twentieth-century world environment that is different from any past age, and a pointer to the future. We must expect alliances to become weaker and less significant, policies of independence and nonalignment to be more widespread, international functional organizations to become more important, ideological differences to decrease under pressure of common and universal demands made upon states, as a result of these basic trends we have observed. We must expect more and more exchanges to take place directly between people and organizations in different countries, and less and less in proportion between governments, as trade, interdependence and communications increase. Even relations between planned economies will be more and more decentralized: industrial units in the Soviet Union will more and more negotiate directly with relevant industrial units in other states.

Student riots occur almost simultaneously in countries far apart. Why? Racial conflict flares up in many different states almost simultaneously. Why? New means of producing things, new ideas, new ambitions and objectives occur. Is this because some great master mind in one government is able to influence people in other states? Or is it because there is a flow of knowledge and ideas that no boundaries can prevent? The billiard-ball model does not answer these questions.

(iv) The twentieth century

Thanks to land, sea and air transport, to postal and telegraphic services, to newspapers and books, to radio and television and to tourism and migration, there is now a world society – a society that comprises peoples everywhere, who know of one another, and who in most cases trade and communicate with one another. Relationships are still restricted: not all people can read and write, only some have radios and television sets. Different languages and the absence of direct visual contacts limit communication, and sometimes personal movements and communications are hampered deliberately by authorities for financial or ideological reasons. However, most barriers are being reduced by technological developments, by the spread of education, and by popular demands for opportunities to be informed of what takes place elsewhere. No matter how different peoples are in culture, social development and material conditions, and no matter how geographically distant from each other, they have today knowledge of what is possible, and share expectations of increased welfare and more direct control over their social circumstances. This communication is now practically universal, even between people who do not read and write, and who do not travel.

This world human society is clearly not a political or an administrative entity. It comprises smaller societies such as states, nations, and local communities, and even smaller social groups such as business organizations, schools and families. World society will never be an integrated whole even in the absence of all restraints on communications. One reason is an administrative one: effective decentralization of decision-making that gives people a sense of participation, and which takes account of local conditions, will increase with the passage of time and not decrease. Another reason is a psychological one. People have a need to identify with others; first the family and kinship group, then wider social groups, then the nation and the state. Very few people are able to identify with world society. Each of these separate social groups is influenced in its behaviour by its own material circumstances including climate, geographical position, available resources and living standards, and by its traditions and culture. Each has its own fears, envies, hopes and ambitions.

Disharmonies among these local and social groups occur when members of different ones are in the one economic or political unit. Class, ideological, ethnic, religious and language differences within a state are a source of conflict within it. Most states comprise these different social groups. Class and ideological differences occur in all societies as a result of social and technological influences. Ethnic, religious and language differences were once introduced by invasions and migrations and are now promoted by the same increased communications that have created world society. These group conflicts within states frequently attract the attention of sympathetic or similar groups in other states, leading to conflicts between states. Indeed, it seems that, in the absence of total equality and participation in political life, different social groups, be they different ideologically, culturally or ethnically, cannot live harmoniously together within any one administrative unit except in those cases in which there are strong majorities and weak minorities, or in which one can effectively coerce and control the other. Where minorities are weak the identity of the majority is not threatened and it can afford to respect and even give generous treatment to a minority.

We will return to a consideration of conflict and merely note here that the existence of separate groups is not necessarily destructive of world society. On the contrary, local loyalties and the personal security provided by identification with family and nation, promote social integration and stability, and a basis on which different social groups can coexist and cooperate within the wider national or world society. There is some evidence that conflict is least likely among groups, be they families or nations, that are themselves well integrated. It is the continued contacts and mutual sympathies of peoples of different nationalities and ideologies that make it possible to speak of a world society.

Somewhere buried in the mass of interactions and influences that affect social units, small and large, is an explanation of relationships in world society, sometimes peaceful, sometimes violent. How do we set about explaining world society, and finding the principles of policy whereby groups can achieve their objectives? There is a history to an explanation of any phenomenon. Gravity, disease and delinquency have throughout time been explained in different ways. Happenings in world society, too, have been explained at different times by different people in different ways. They have been explained by suggesting that men are violent or aggressive by nature, or by the belief that the separation of world society into states of different size and power creates a condition that allows ordinary competition and conflict to develop into violence. But human nature and the existence of sovereign states of unequal influence and power do not satisfactorily explain many features of our present-day world society. Human aggressiveness can be shown to be a response to circumstances – it is not an 'instinct' that must find some outlet. Perhaps in the days when kings and princes ruled, and when there were lands to be populated and unclaimed resources to be discovered and exploited, there were conditions that stimulated competitive acquisition and even aggressiveness. Rivalries between states no doubt then dominated world events. But today we are living in a world almost totally explored and claimed, in which there are limited opportunities for state acquisition. It is a world in which communications have brought about relationships among people and groups in addition to relationships among states. Ideological thinking, tourism, trade, science, the radio and religion jump state boundaries. Perhaps these relationships that cut across state boundaries are even now more influential in world society than the relations that exist among states at a formal government level. Certainly they will become more and more influential with further increases in communications and learning. Any explanation of world society must take fully into account transactions of all kinds between peoples directly, in addition to relationships among governments.

Approached in this way the study of world society is not one that is separate from the study of different societies that comprise world society. Any separation between municipal politics and international politics is an artificial and probably a misleading one. The conflict between Nigeria and Biafra was a communal one and also an international one, as is the conflict between racial groups in Rhodesia and South Africa. Problems of poverty within a state are merely part of the wider problem of inequality of incomes in world society. States and state boundaries are real, and they have widespread consequences; but there are important influences in world society that can be considered without taking state boundaries into account. We can understand world society only by examining all relationships, not just those that take place between governments. It could be, for example, that the origins and explanations of inter-state conflict are to be found in political relationships within states, or within the processes by which decisions affecting other states are taken within states. As has been suggested already, terms such as 'world society', and 'world politics' are more appropriate as descriptions of what has been termed in the past 'international relations'. 'International relations' comprises a more restricted study, namely the study of the transactions between sovereign entities, in particular the legal relationships that exist between states.

(v) The cobweb model

The conventional map of the world is a physical one: it shows geographical relationships, over which are sometimes drawn political boundaries. It does not tell us much about processes or behaviour. The same proportional space and importance are given to seas and deserts as are given to ports and cities. There do exist diagrammatic maps that tell us where populations are concentrated, where resources are to be found, how many newspapers are read and other information such as this.[15] But even these do not give us much information about behaviour, or more particularly, about transactions and links that exist. We are familiar with maps of the world showing air and shipping routes. What we really need to have, either in map form or conceptually, is an image of world society that shows behaviour by showing these linkages. If we could superimpose on successive sheets of transparent paper air-passenger movements per week, telegraphic flows, ethnic and language relations, movements of scholars, technical advisers, migration, tourism, and all other transactions, we would begin to build up a picture of relationships which would help to explain behaviour in world society far better than traditional maps. Maps were designed to show people how to get from point A to point B. They are useful for this purpose. But they have been used for purposes other than this. They have had the effect of creating in our minds this geographical image of world society. What we need is a map or concept that tells us something about behaviour. The difference is like the difference between a set of photos of a car showing its headlamps and other details, and the type of diagram an electrical engineer would draw showing the wiring links within the electrical system. We cannot understand a car by looking at it. Its processes need to be analysed, and then we can understand it, and remedy any failures.

If we had been brought up with such maps on the wall, if we were not so consciously aware of states whenever we looked at a map of the world, and best of all, if we had never seen an ordinary map of the world, we would think far more in terms of world society and far less in terms of a system of states. We would approach closer to a realistic model of world society.

An easy way to think about this second model is by use of the concept of 'system'. A system exists when there are relationships or transactions between units of the same set. There is a system of states, and there are also transactions between businessmen, traders, research workers, television stations, drug peddlers, students and others. There are systems or linkages such as those created by amateur radio enthusiasts, by peoples with the same ideological or religious outlooks, by scientists exchanging papers and meeting together, by people behaving in their different ways. It is the total of these which we need to see as a behavioural map of the world. In this model contacts are not only at the boundaries of sovereign states, but between points within each.

We have gone to a great deal of trouble and expense over the years to map rivers and mountains, sea depths and ocean currents; but we have not as yet been sufficiently interested in social and political studies to map the behaviour of men. In most cases we do not even have the basic information required. When we look at the ordinary physical map we have to impose on it our own personal knowledge. For example, we may know where populations are massed, and where there are deserts. We have our own ideas, usually inaccurate, about which populations are friendly, aggressive, backward, developed, black, white, yellow, and perhaps we have a vague idea which are Muslim, Hindu, Christian and Buddhist. We have some idea where different commodities are produced, where trade flows, and which are the most used shipping and air lanes. We rely on our personal knowledge. There are some physical maps which superimpose accurately some of this information for us, and even some diagrammatical 'maps' or graphs which show comparative figures, such as percentages of total world wheat produced in various countries.[16] The few maps of this kind that do exist are helpful. They give us a new perspective on the world, and help us to see at a glance what otherwise can be understood only by looking at statistics (see Figs. 1–3).

We still have difficulty in conceptualizing world society, first because these 'maps' are inadequate, and second because by their nature they are misleading. They are inadequate not only in the sense that data are available which have not been presented in this form, and in the sense that relevant data have never been obtained. They are inadequate in terms of their analytical content. A population figure for a country, even an average population per square mile, does not tell us those things about distribution which would make a glance at a map meaningful. In theory it should be possible to put a dot wherever anyone is; in practice it is possible to do this by taking 10,000 people as a unit. Then we would have the rudimentary basis of a human behavioural map. A next step would be to differentiate between race, language and other differences in more and more detail in a series of superimposed maps. A further step would be to examine relationships between these sets or different groups of people. Take, for example, Malaysia. There are many different sets: Malays, Chinese, anti-communist and pro-communist Malays and Chinese, traditionally-oriented and religious Muslims and other Malays, Chinese business-men, and so on. Each of these sets has its own values and interests, and therefore its own external sympathies. Some Chinese look to China, and others to Taiwan, some Malays are nationalist and some look to Indonesia and other Muslim countries for support in any possible confrontation with Chinese. These sets can be represented by interlocking circles: one person can be Chinese by birth, regard himself as a Malay nationalist, a businessman, British educated and oriented and anti-communist. He must be placed in an area in which the circles representing all these sets overlap (see Fig. 4).

If we considered neighbouring Indonesia in the same way, we would find similar sets. Putting the two alongside each other it would at once become clear that any alliance between the two would be seen

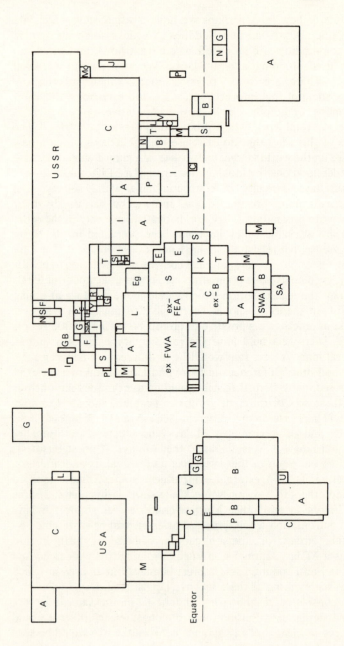

Fig. 1. The countries of the world, according to surface area

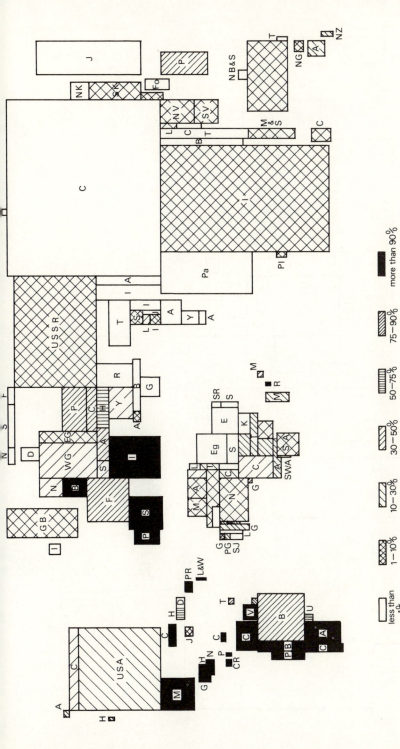

Fig. 2. Percentage of baptized Catholics, by country

less than 1%	1—10%	10—30%	30—50%	50—75%	75—90%	more than 90%

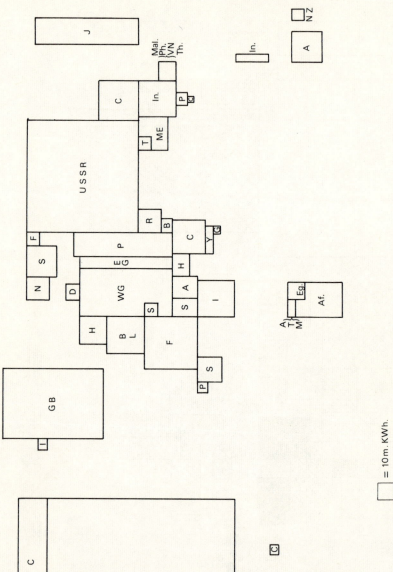

= 10 m. KWh.

Fig. 3. Energy consumption

Fig. 4. Sets represented by interlocking circles

as a threat to some sets in each. Chinese, for example, would see such an alliance as a Malayan threat to them. We could reasonably assume, just by looking at these sets, that attempts to establish regional arrangements would lead to increased internal tension and conflict within each political unit. Just by analysing existing data we could come to some important hypotheses about behaviour. We are just beginning to do this – despite the urgent need to solve the problems of world society.

Even though our existing data were fully used in these ways, we would still not have a map of human behaviour. These are data based on state statistics: state populations, state trade, state classifications. We are interested in transactions across state boundaries of which states have little knowledge, and certainly no statistics – the sympathies Jewish people have for one another, the transmission of values attached to participation in decision-making, the way in which people of the same tribe or ethnic group identify with each other across state boundaries, and the flow of ideas. We are also interested in the direction of flow: there are state statistics giving the flow of mail across state boundaries, but not the direction of these flows. One example of a flow map is Fig. 5. This kind of map is necessary for many behavioural relationships.

We would begin to get nearer to such a concept of world society if we were to map it without reference to political boundaries, and indeed, without reference to any physical boundaries. We are not particularly concerned with boundaries, except insofar as they affect behaviour by reducing transactions and communications among people. We are concerned with behaviour – boundaries or no boundaries. If we were to start with a clean sheet of paper and plot people in various sets, their transport and communications, we would, in fact, create a map some of which would be recognizable as parts of the physical map of the world. One difference would be that seas and deserts would look the same. We could build on this additional information, perhaps by a series of transparent sheets, and finally superimpose political boundaries.

Communications are a good starting point because they are an important means of transactions or links between people. It is communications or links between units that create systems. A useful map of the world could be drawn by plotting on a blank piece of paper all post offices. In some cases the system links would form clusters recognizable as a country. In others, for example, some areas of the Middle East, it would immediately seem that there were as many or more transactions across boundaries as within. If we could map all movements and communications in world society we would find some ethnic groups communicating across state boundaries as though they did not exist, as, for example, between Somalia and Kenya, and between many Western European countries. This would give us a picture of some important aspects of behaviour which a physical map cannot give. Conceptually we could extend this to include all transactions and links, even those we cannot quantify and map, such as ideological sympathies, and the hidden transactions of international corporations and international institutions of all kinds. In practice there are so many direct communications or systems that a world map which represented them would look like a mass of cobwebs superimposed on one another, strands converging at some points more than others, and being concentrated between some points more than between others. The boundaries of states would be hidden from view.

Which is the more representative model of the world – the world of continents, islands and states or the world of transactions? This is not a superficial question. There are two different models or images presented. If we adopt the nation-state one we will use the language of relations between states and their relevant power, and have one set of solutions to problems of conflict and world organization. If we adopt the transactions one we will use a different language to describe world society, and have a different set of solutions to world problems. For example, we will be greatly concerned with political and social conditions within states because it is these which, in this model, determine relationships in world society, including relations between states.

Let us dwell on this a little more. The model we have at the back of our minds determines our interpretation of events, our theories and our policies. For example, the billiard-ball model is a power model – world society is seen to be organized by the relative power of each unit. There are matters of domestic jurisdiction of no concern to others, not even the United Nations. There are legal political entities that have a right to protect themselves and to expect assistance from others, including the United Nations, if they are threatened, even though they have no popular support – no legitimized status. Collective security is the means of preventing 'aggression'. Economic development is the means to social and political stability.

The model depicting transactions invites a different approach to world problems. The source of conflict between states is in internal

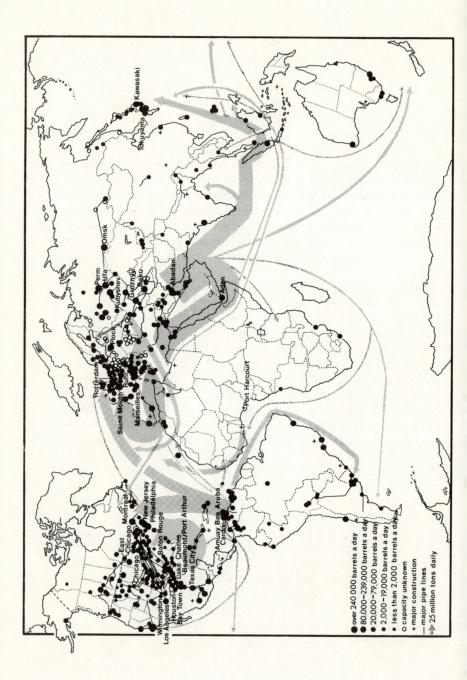

Kawasaki
Tokuyama
Omsk
Perm
Ufa
Kuybyshev
Groznyy
Baku
Abadan
Rotterdam
Moskva
Aden
Seine Mouth
Ruhr
Marseilles
Port Harcourt
Montreal
East Chicago
New Jersey
Chicago
Philadelphia
Baton Rouge
Lake Charles
Beaumont/Port Arthur
Texas City
Amuay Bay
Cardon
Aruba
Wilmington
Los Angeles
Houston
Bay Town

● over 240 000 barrels a day
● 80,000–239,000 barrels a day
● 20,000–79,000 barrels a day
• 2,000–19,000 barrels a day
• less than 2,000 barrels a day
○ capacity unknown
+ major construction
— major pipe lines
⇒ 25 million tons daily

politics, in failures by states to adjust to altering conditions, in the struggle of states to preserve their institutions, and in the conflict between states and systems that cut across state boundaries. Conflict cannot be prevented by external coercion, or by great power threats. Communal conflict – race, religious, ideological – invites sympathies across state boundaries and promotes international conflict. The role of authorities is to assist in the making of adjustments to altering conditions so that conflict between interests within the state, and the wider world systems, do not occur. Development and stability must rest on internal conditions or political organization, that is, a high degree of participation so that authorities are strongly legitimized. In accordance with this model, a form of world government cannot rest on collective security, and must be based on the transactions inherent in functional organizations that are, by their nature, universal in potential membership. Viable political units can be very small, provided there is a high level of transactions with the wider environment. Communications, and not power, are the main organizing influence in world society.

There is an important practical question raised here. An image of world society that comprises separate state entities, each potentially hostile to others, leads understandably to defensive policies. Is the image a realistic one, or are the conflicts that occur and seem to validate the image merely the consequences of our having this image? An image of world society that depicts transactions, controlled and regulated by local state and international authorities, with a view to securing the maximum benefits from interdependence without loss of security, leads reasonably to integrative policies. Is the image a realistic one, or are the functional arrangements, world corporations and other evidences that seem to validate the image merely the consequence of us having this image? It is possible that the cobweb image is the realistic one, except insofar as lack of confidence has created the one comprising separate and fearful entities. Thus created it becomes part of our perceived reality.

(vi) The systems approach
The systems approach, which the cobweb model depicts, has some methodological advantages. It is a means of seeing wholes – the whole of the electrical system or the braking system. It is a means of detailed analysis without losing sight of total interactions. We can see the whole of the front or side of a car by looking at it; but what we are seeing are parts of some of its systems. We cannot make any

behavioural analysis. It is true that the electrical system is not the whole car. But systems and sub-systems are wholes in themselves, acting within their environment of other systems and sub-systems.[17]

A systems approach helps in clarifying our notion of regionalism. Sometimes the reason for regional studies has been because a scholar has an interest in a set of countries, for example those in Asia, Africa or Latin America. Indeed, traditional studies were regional studies in the sense that they dealt primarily with the policies of European states. This approach to regionalism is, therefore, very little different from ordinary historical and descriptive studies of particular states and their relationships.

Some scholars have thought it would be useful to study regions as such rather than the foreign policies of particular states. The reason is that 'regionalism' has been thought to offer a means of international organization, that is, a way of promoting security or development. A theory of regionalism has developed just as has a theory of functionalism.

Does the study of regionalism, as distinct from the study of states within a region, give us some special insights into world society, or some suggested approaches to problems of peace and development?

Before we try to answer this question we have to state what we mean by a region – because the definition we take influences the answer. If we define a region in geographical terms we are really dealing with regionalism as the study of certain countries within a given geographical area. There is probably little that we can learn from such studies that cannot be learned from traditional studies of diplomatic history and relations between states. If, on the other hand, we adopt a systems approach and define a region in terms of systems, there is more to learn. Let us take the geographical area of South East Asia as a focus area. We are concerned with interactions. We perceive systems of relationships, trading, language, religion (that takes us into the Muslim areas of the Middle East and the Buddhist area of Asia), ethnic (which includes relations with China and India), ideological, strategic (which includes the USA and the UK) and others.

On examination we find that the states in the region are multi-set – that is, there are many overlapping communities of interest within each one. There are Muslims, Chinese, communists, anti-communists, and so on. The relations between the states include relations (sympathies and common values) between Chinese and Chinese, Muslim and Muslim, and so on. The relations between the states are not just the formal relations between the authorities in control of each state.

This is more important in understanding behaviour in world society than would first appear to be the case. Why have these states failed to arrive at security arrangements? Why do they fear 'communist (Chinese) aggression'? Why are there serious internal tensions over language and religion? The fact is that each is loosely integrated. The overlapping sets of interest create a precarious political balance. Any arrangements amongst them would upset that balance. We have seen already that a regional security agreement between Indonesia and Malaysia would be interpreted by the indigenous Chinese as a plot against them. They would look for external support, leading others to do the same – and before long there would be foreign intervention and perhaps international conflict arising out of this attempted regional integration. By determining the sets in each unit, and by analysing system relationships within the region, we can begin to understand some of the interactions that are not revealed by an examination of the states one by one. This is a systems approach applied to a regional study.

What we need is a notion of 'effective distance'. Geographical proximity is but one influence. Asian countries, in the colonial period, traded with and had most links with European states. Shipping, telegraphic and other communications were more intensive between Asian states and their metropolitan authorities than between each other. So communications are another influence in determining effective distance. The cultural, religious, ethnic and ideological ties are yet others. Regionalism as a geographical concept is misleading. The members of the British Commonwealth possibly have been effectively 'closer' than countries within any one geographical area.

Not only are the possibilities and restraints on integration revealed; such an analysis also suggests where external involvement is likely to occur. For example, the Malaysian situation could develop as the Nigerian one did. The Chinese are a very large minority, and their economic position is resented by Malays. Chinese resent Malay privileges written into the constitution. In the event of a serious racial clash Chinese could concentrate in some areas for self-protection. A next step could be an attempt at secession. On the Nigerian precedent, the Soviet Union might assist in maintaining unity, and Britain might try to maintain its presence. All this is speculative and perhaps unlikely. But we come nearer to both an analysis of a current situation and forecasting possible outcomes if we take into account systems links in addition to the current statements of government policy. So, too, in Africa. A careful analysis of tribal language, cultural, commercial, communication and other such links would give some insights into relationships that are not revealed in formal statements of government policy, and which can destroy governments and transform states. Unfortunately, while diplomatic history is usually well documented, we still lack systems data. Statistics are state based: a lot of work is required to produce systems data when the systems cut across state boundaries.

A systems approach does not provide a model of world society. It is a way of thinking: it is a means of breaking up world society into wholes small enough to be analysed. It is an alternative to breaking up world society by dealing with aspects of the whole – economic, psychological or political. It provides a vocabulary which is applicable at all behavioural levels. It provides an alternative perspective of world society: one that is less concerned with geographical relationships and more concerned with behavioural links.

Systems comprise linkages between units of the same set. Students, members of a political party, telephone components are each in their own set. Apples are a set and pears another. But apples and pears are in one set made up of fruit. The 'level' of set can be raised in this way. Similarly it can be 'lowered'. Apples can be separated into a set of green ones and a set of red ones, or eating and cooking. Consequently there can be systems levels.

This enables us to connect systems and roles. A student is in one system in a class, in another on the playing field. The same unit can be in a different set because of a different role. So with larger social groups and states. In one role a state is an ally, in another an antagonist. In alliances states are expected to ignore differences that arise out of different interests, and the greater powers dominate. In a nonaligned system each unit behaves as it thinks best and adopts its own policies in respect of each situation. Nonalignment is a system in which there is an acceptance of different role behaviour by others.

One of the most difficult problems in political analysis, especially at the world level, is to determine where analogy ends and real description begins. 'States, like men are aggressive.' Is this mere analogy, or is it something more because states in fact include men? Systems analysis is of some help in solving this problem. All men have legs, but states do not have legs. There are set features and systems features. We have to make sure that we are confining our attention to system features if we want to employ the study of one set of things or people to the study of another. 'All men live in and respond to an environ-ment' is a system feature of the behaviour of men. All states also exist in and respond to an environment. There will be some responses of men and social groups that will help us in understanding the behaviour of larger groups and even states.

Because we can use systems thinking in these ways we can take advantage of research in many behavioural studies. We can examine conditions in which coercion and deterrence are effective, and others in which they fail. For example, we may find that coercion is effective when (a) the behaviour required is known precisely, and (b) the value of the institution within which it takes place is greater than the immediate goal against which the coercion is directed. If we find out something about coercion and deterrence in ordinary social life, we may then be in a position to say that sanctions against Rhodesia will be effective if (a) what we require of them is stated in precise terms, and (b) the value to Rhodesians of the British Commonwealth or the United Nations is greater than the value they attach to their discrimi-natory policies.

Clearly one can never be certain that one has not confused set and system features: one can never be sure that analogy and reality have not been confused. But a systems approach at least helps to guide and to stimulate thinking, and to enable us to make the greatest possible use of work in other disciplines. Important also is that it helps to remind us of the 'whole' of world society. It will be recalled that we commenced this discussion by saying that the study of world society was important because it was the study of the whole in which parts can be examined. Systems thinking, systems concepts and language, enable us to break up this unmanageable whole into 'wholes' of sub-systems without losing the wider perspective.

(vii) The orientation model

A model or image that highlights systems and ignores relations between sovereign states and the power they exercise in world society is misleading, just as the billiard-ball model of state relations is unreal. No drawn diagram is possible that can show both at the same time. The difference aspects of world society to which each model draws attention are in reality incompatible to some degree. States live in and respond to a changing world environment that is more and more dominated by transactions of all kinds over which they have, indi-vidually and collectively, little control. States are sometimes in conflict with systems, both the systems within their territorial jurisdiction, and systems that are international and only partly within their jurisdiction. World society appears to be at a transition stage at which it is neither a world comprising only states, nor a world comprising only systems. The models are, therefore, useful only in the sense that they draw attention to some features and force us to ask ourselves important questions. To what extent will communications further influence international relations? Are state boundaries becoming less important, and are the functions and responsibilities of governments changing? Will more new states emerge accompanied by increased cross-national transactions? Is the behaviour of great powers changing? Do conflicts among systems, and systems and states, lead to conflict between states? To what extent can the operations of states be carried out by functional institutions and a further growth of international systems?

These are questions suggested to us by two models, two different images of world society. Being derived from models they are expressed in conceptual terms like systems and conflict among systems, that make them sound out of touch with the historical reality of conflict between states. Yet our models were derived from our observations of reality: the billiard-ball one did not cope with the consequences of communications, so we had to create a cobweb one, in addition. We should, therefore, be able to express these questions in terms of real situations and political experience. We should be able, by using these models and the questions they suggest, to come closer to the basic forces and problems of world society.

Because these models are so different, and direct attention to different aspects of society without any means of evaluating the relative influence of states and systems, they are unsatisfactory. Furthermore, they are structural and institutional models and as such suggest only some questions, and direct attention to the need for empirical investigation only in respect of systems and states.

When we look at world society less abstractly, and more as perceived by the individual, the apparent incompatibilities between these two models diminish. This is due to our ability to switch from one orientation to the other according to our perception and interest. As Kelman has remarked after observing the existence of a series of transnational societies: .

'The new developments do not require a displacement of national loyalties by loyalty to transnational institutions or organizations. They do, however, imply a tolerance for multiple loyalties, for permitting the development of transnational loyalties alongside of national ones. But there is no necessary conflict between the two, for multiple sets of loyalties are, in principle, completely compatible with one another, as long as groups to which they are directed serve different functions and apply to different domains of a person's behaviour.'[18]

From a structural point of view Kelman advances a modification of the systems model. 'A major implication of the new developments is that, in important ways, we are living in a transnational, global society – or perhaps, to be more accurate, in a series of transnational, global societies. That is, what is evolving is not a global society in the sense of a single unit, defined on a territorial basis, but different ways of forming transnational units to carry out a variety of specific functions or to give expression to a variety of specific values and tastes. These global societies are taking shape in addition to, not instead of, the national societies to which we belong.'[19]

PART TWO

Analysis of World Society

5. *Perceptions*

Where is the starting point of analysis of world society? Is it the study of history, of geographical and commercial relations, of particular powerful governments, of international institutions, or of systems? These are all descriptive studies, sometimes involving our personal interpretations. We need to delve deeper into behaviour.

(i) Perceived relationships

Social relationships are perceived relationships. Friendship, cooperation, hostility, envy, anger and aggressiveness are attitudes that are perceived by individuals and groups. The emphasis is on 'perceived'. What is perceived is not necessarily the attitude that is being displayed. A friendly gesture is sometimes observed and interpreted as open or disguised hostility. Cooperation is sometimes interpreted as a means of acquiring an advantage. In business and in social life one is never quite sure whether one is observing and interpreting behaviour as it is intended to be.

Even a third party who is not directly involved in a relationship cannot be certain about the attitudes of the other parties. Sometimes he can arrange a situation in which he can test the attitudes of those he is observing, and in this way be less doubtful about his observations. Teachers and parents sometimes find themselves in a position in which they have to make judgements about the behaviour of young people, and all they have to guide them is what they are told by others, and what they have observed for themselves in a variety of situations. Their judgements tend to be accepted as valid because they are in positions of authority. Their judgement can, nevertheless, be misleading and false.

Relations between nations and states are of this 'subjective' character. It is impossible to know what relationships really are, that is what exactly those concerned mean them to be. All that can be known is what they are seen to be by the persons and groups

55

concerned, and by others looking on. The judgements of more powerful states tend to be accepted, not because of experience or wisdom, but because of their authority and power.

It follows that our social problems do not arise necessarily out of the aggressiveness, hostility, or other characteristics of people and nations, as is often assumed. They may arise out of the observations and interpretations that are made by others. A defensive gesture by a person who thinks he may be attacked is apt to be interpreted by others as preparation for an attack on them, thus leading them to act defensively, or even to attack. Consequently, we are led to ask the question, which is the source of relationships in world society, the real nature and behaviour of men and states, or false interpretations of their behaviour? As soon as one asks a question like this a much more searching question is suggested: what is the real nature and behaviour of men and states? are nations aggressive, or do they act aggressively as a result of their beliefs that others are aggressive?

A study of diplomatic history and the thinking of philosophers shows that the assumed aggressiveness of men and nations has been thought to be the prime cause of international conflict, and the major problem of world society. Some anthropologists and biologists have accepted the evidence of history, and have looked for explanations of aggressiveness. They have traced human behaviour from primitive forms. They can demonstrate circumstances under which animals and men are aggressive. Overcrowding, competition for scarce food, protection of territory, and the usual processes of survival by living on other species have been put forward as fundamental causes of conflict in world society, even in contemporary world society. 'Survival of the fittest' has been an idea that has seemed a good general explanation of animal and human behaviour. On the basis of an idea such as this it can be argued that every nation will seek to be as powerful as possible, and that the structure of world society is the result of the relative power positions of states. It can be argued that the greater states decide the general nature of world society, and to a large degree the behaviour of the smaller states that are under their direct or indirect control.

This kind of explanation of world society seemed entirely reasonable in days when large areas of the earth's surface were still uninhabited, or if already inhabited were being explored and exploited by those nations that had developed more rapidly and had acquired means of transport and weapons with which to control others. There was competition in exploration and colonization among the more powerful states that were intent upon acquiring more territory. There were invasions in Asia and South East Asia before Europeans discovered these areas, and then there were European invasions. Acquisition and power were clearly most important influences that determined how less developed societies would develop, the rate of exploitation of resources, the directions of trade, and generally the structure of world society. It is little wonder that men who were observing and thinking about nations and how they behaved gave attention to power, and especially to military power, and to the personal characteristics of leaders who were prepared to use what power was at their disposal to increase the territory and influence of their nations.

Our world is a different one, at least in some respects, and to some degree. Areas that were made into colonies by powerful states have now, with a few exceptions, become independent. There are few new regions to be explored. In due course there will be an even greater interest than at present in the regions of the North and South Poles, and there will be very great interest in the regions of the sea beds and of outer space. Only the technically developed states will be able to explore and exploit these. Failing some international controls competition in exploration and acquisition could occur again. But at present power and influence are directed mainly toward maintaining 'spheres of influence'; the United States and the Soviet Union in particular, and increasingly China, are anxious to maintain security areas, and also to preserve or expand their trading and cultural interests.

There are many other differences between our world and that which was being observed by scholars in the past who believed that relative power satisfactorily explained the structure and processes of world society. There is 'nuclear deterrence' which seems to prevent or at least restrain great powers from coming into direct conflict with each other. This has many side effects: great powers are reluctant to become involved directly with each other in any form of military conflict for fear that nuclear weapons might ultimately be employed. There is the expanded 'third world' of new states, especially in Asia and Africa. Their influence is increasing in international councils, and they are beginning to make more and more demands for equality of trading opportunities, and for the elimination of practices that discriminate against them. There is the rise of the 'welfare state' in which people insist upon resources and opportunities being more fairly distributed, and upon increased expenditure on material and cultural needs even at the expense of defence. We have already noted a universal communication which enables peoples everywhere to know what others are achieving and thinking. There is, as a result, a rapid spread of new expectations or 'values', which leads peasants in Asia to demand a greater return for their work and to rebel against systems by which landlords retain a high proportion of the products of the land. There is a universal demand for the right to take part in making decisions at local, national and international levels, leading to demands by minority national groups for independence, to demands for votes by women, to demands by students to be consulted in matters that affect them, and to demands by small and developing states to be brought into the making of decisions on financial and trading matters that determine their welfare. Indeed, while those drafting the United Nations Charter in 1945 placed greatest emphasis on security and the Security Council, today there is a far greater interest in human rights and the work of the Assembly and the Economic and Social Council.

Perhaps, then, we should be thinking about world society differently, and we should be trying to find explanations that better fit modern conditions than those that explained all state behaviour by reference to the power of states. Should we not be examining the demands being made by people who have no 'power' in the military sense, but who are most powerful by reason of their numbers, and by reason of the acknowledged justice of their demands. We have a new set of problems now. They are not problems of competition between powerful states. They are problems of racial discrimination, underdevelopment, inequalities of incomes, security in conditions in which communications and transport bring nations closer together, and problems that arise because we now attach great value to education, culture, independence, and the right to be ourselves and to develop.

It might be argued that despite these changes governments act in much the same way as they did a century ago. To some degree this is true. Diplomats and politicians responsible for foreign policy, and people generally, still think in power terms, and still assume that other states are aggressive. Just by assuming that the world society is as it was, and acting accordingly, some of the conditions of the past are being maintained. Because it is assumed that states are still competing for scarce resources and seeking to acquire more territory, each nation tries to defend itself. This defence appears to others to be preparation for aggression, thus seeming to justify the belief that each state is potentially aggressive. The old pattern is perpetuated. This in practice happens to a very large extent. National policies are probably more based on the assumptions that states make about the behaviour of each other than on the actual motives and intentions of each state.

The problem of those engaged in the study of world society is to find, first, how those who make decisions see world society, second, its 'real' nature, that is the motivations of states, why they behave as they do, and third, the guidelines on which to base government policies that will bridge the gap between perception and reality – and thus avoid self-defeating consequences of policy.

Whereas traditionally the aggressiveness of men and states has been assumed or has been the object of observation and comment, let us now concentrate more upon the way in which behaviour is observed and interpreted. We may find that aggressiveness is natural and inevitable, just as though it were a human instinct. On the other hand, we may find it has been thought to exist but does not in fact exist, or we may find that aggressiveness exists only in certain circumstances which provoke it. Let us give humanity the benefit of the doubt for the moment, and see to what extent we can explain world society and the behaviour of states by paying attention in the first instance to the way in which behaviour is observed and interpreted.

(ii) Problems of visual perception

There are two sets of influences which determine interpretations of reality. There are perceptions, which may be accurate or inaccurate, that arise out of the biological structures of our sensory organs, especially the eyes, and the habits that we acquire in using them. 'Perspective' is an example. There are, in addition, perceptions that result from our emotional and learned attitudes which guide us in the selection of information, and in the reassembly of information which we have. Racial prejudice is an example. Let us first examine visual perception, and especially the difficulties we have in observing accurately. We will find that we are likely to make all manner of mistakes, not through social attitudes and acquired prejudices, but just because our biological mechanisms and the habits we form lead us to make mistakes. Then we can turn to other misperceptions that occur because of emotional and acquired prejudices, or myths and theories which we have learned.

The easiest way to do this is by reference to simple diagrams. We know that, due to the way in which the eye is constructed, objects look smaller the further away they are. A major problem for the artist is to obtain realistic perspective. We are accustomed to perspective. A set of straight railway lines converge to a point in the distance (Fig. 6).

We are so accustomed to this representation of distance that when distance figures are drawn the same size as nearer ones we think that the distant ones are larger (Fig. 7).

Other examples show how we are misled in our judgement just by reason of accompanying lines. Vertical lines drawn parallel appear to be curved when placed on radiating background lines (Fig. 8).

Horizontal lines that are the same length appear to be of different lengths when accompanied by converging lines (Fig. 9).

The effect of environment or concurrent circumstances on our observations is very great. Student riots in England in 1968 were criticized because they were thought to be inspired by a few irresponsible 'extremists' who were probably 'communists', while student riots that took place at the same time in Poland were welcomed in England as evidence of a responsible and liberal student reaction against an oppressive government. From Poland, English riots probably seemed responsible, while their own seemed inspired by some foreign nations. The riots could have had similar causes and could have been led by similar students.

Not only are we apt to distort reality in some environmental circumstances, we are also apt to see things which in reality cannot exist. It is possible to draw what appears to be a triangle composed of rectangular pieces of wood (Fig. 10). At first sight it looks real enough. Then when we look carefully it becomes apparent that there are three dimensions and not just two – where the sides should stand on a base cut at 45 degrees, they stand on one cut at a right angle. The test is to take some rectangular blocks and see if such a triangle can be made out of them.

One suspects that many of our images of other people and other nations are like this: we have 'impossible' ideas, but they seem to us reasonable because we are not aware of the unreasonable features included in our image.

Not only are we capable of seeing things that cannot exist; we can also see the same thing in more ways than one. In Fig. 11 can be seen an old lady or a young girl. Some people see one, some the other. Who is seeing correctly – that is, what is really there? Both images are 'correct'. It is difficult to see one when you have first seen the other, but easy to see both when once you have looked hard and seen both.

Say the image is a pictorial representation of the behaviour of

Fig. 6. The Poncho illusion – in the real world? The railway lines are the same as in the illusion figure (Fig. 9 on page 62), but here they are clearly perspective lines – parallels converging with distance. The illusion still holds

Fig. 7. The four men are actually the same size; evidently perspective in some way expands the apparently more distant men

Fig. 8 (*left*). The Hering illusion. This striking bending of the verticals is produced by the radiating background lines

Fig. 9. The Poncho illusion. The upper of the two horizontals appears the longer: the distortion is produced by the converging lines

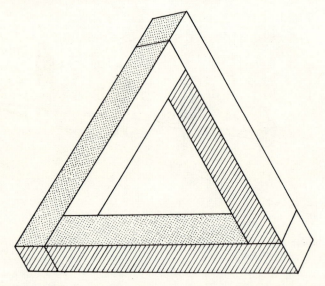

Fig. 10. An 'impossible object'; this triangle cannot exist (after L. S. and R. Penrose, *Brit. Journ. Psychol.* 49 (1958), 31)

Fig. 11. Which is it – an old woman with chin sunk in wrap, or the heroine of an early twentieth-century romantic novel, her chin held high?

China, America, Egypt or Israel. Which is reality, a peaceful or an aggressive state? Depending on which features you look at, you can see one or the other.

Even more disturbing is the fact that when we are ignorant about a situation it makes no sense, and looks just a muddled condition. Fig. 12 below looks like ink blots. If you look carefully you see parts fit into a recognizable pattern, and a man's head appears (Fig. 13). When we have just a few scraps of information about other people and nations we have an image of muddle, or of lack of organization, or perhaps the domination of one person who happens to be in the news, but no clear picture of the whole.

These are all examples of visual perception and misperception. Our other senses, hearing and touch, play the same tricks. Sometimes one sense communicates one message, and another another, and we do not know which to believe. On television soft music tells us to watch for a love scene, and quick, sharp, loud music indicates a horse chase in a 'western'. How confused we would be if a love scene were accompanied by rolling drums. Press reports of world events confuse us in the same way. A visible arms race in the Middle East or between the United States and the Soviet Union tells one story, and the words of leaders declaring their peaceful intentions tell another.

We have our own ways of sorting out conflicting and different information. Two groups of students were shown the same objects, but each was given a different description of them (Fig. 14). They were then required to draw what they had been shown. Each group drew an object like the description given, but not as they saw them. This kind of thing happens to all of us. We read in the papers about people, countries and political leaders, and we tend to think about them more in terms of descriptions given than in terms of our own knowledge of the countries and of the peoples whom we have met in them.

It does not follow that because we have false visual images we have false non-visual images or false ideas. It is possible that our reasoned thinking is less subject to error than our visual perception. To some extent this is so. Once we are aware of the tricks our senses can play on us, we can employ our reason to prevent being tricked. Once we know how environment affects our interpretation, we can guard against false judgements. But we have to learn to be on our guard. If we are aware of the dangers of propaganda, inadequate information and prejudice, we are in a position to analyse in detail and check on our perception. When we are studying the policy of a country, when

Fig. 12. The hidden man (after P. B. Porter, in *The Am. Journ. of Psychol.* 67 (1954), 550)

Fig. 13. The hidden man revealed

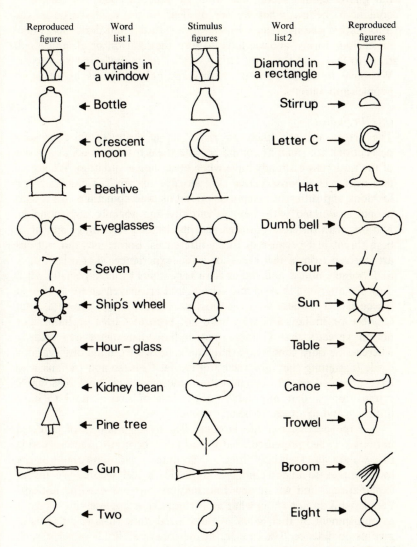

Reproduced figure	Word list 1	Stimulus figures	Word list 2	Reproduced figures
	← Curtains in a window		Diamond in a rectangle →	
	← Bottle		Stirrup →	
	← Crescent moon		Letter C →	
	← Beehive		Hat →	
	← Eyeglasses		Dumb bell →	
	← Seven		Four →	
	← Ship's wheel		Sun →	
	← Hour-glass		Table →	
	← Kidney bean		Canoe →	
	← Pine tree		Trowel →	
	← Gun		Broom →	
	← Two		Eight →	

Fig. 14. Ambiguous figures (after L. Carmichael *et al.* in *Journ. of Exp. Psychol.* vol. 15, p. 80)

we are trying to see whether it is aggressive or not, we have to be on our guard against seeing just what we expect to see. We cannot be content to believe what we see or hear unless we have tested the information against reality in some way. In the half dark things take on curious forms, and we have to turn the light on or go and touch them to find what they are. This is 'reality testing' of our visual sense. We have to find means of 'reality testing' our ideas about other peoples and nations.

(iii) Prejudice

The errors we are likely to make as a result of false sensory perceptions are small as compared with the errors we make as a result of the notions we already have when observing a situation. We are all to some extent conservative. We do not like to see change. New fashions and different behaviour offend us, and sometimes we regard people associated with them as morally and socially objectionable. Nations with different customs and institutions sometimes appear to be a threat just because of these differences. Sometimes our notions are derived from a few cases, or a few experiences that others have had. Some Chinese and Indians are very industrious, especially when they are migrants in Asia and Africa, and are driven on by a sense of insecurity. It is these who are most observed by people who are not Chinese or Indian, and who have not been to China or India. The notion spreads that Chinese and Indians are aggressive traders, whereas the only conclusion that can be drawn from the observations made (assuming they are accurate) is that Chinese and Indians who have migrated tend to be energetic tradesmen. The more reasonable proposition is that migrants – regardless of race – tend to have initiative and to appear to be aggressive.

A large part of our life is controlled by all manner of untested notions – called prejudices, old wives' tales, or myths. One reason is that we are all essentially insecure. So many conditions about us are too complex to understand, yet we need to feel secure. We invent explanations, and we fit new information into our existing notions. People who do not know what an earthquake is are likely to regard it as punishment by their gods. We also need some rules to guide us to give us confidence. The peasant farmer obeys all kinds of rules, such as planting at certain phases of the moon. Agricultural societies indulge in elaborate ceremonies to ensure a good season. When we do not know we tend to invent – and everything must in some way fit in with past experience. In dreams we can mix up impossible sequences of events quite happily – all kinds of things that have happened recently that are not really connected. But when we are awake and start to analyse our dreams we see how mixed they were. Sometimes we are no less mixed up in our conscious thinking without being aware of it. We go through life with all manner of curious ideas that one by one are shown to be false as science tests them. Does cancer occur in people who eat the green part of potatoes, and are poorer people less intelligent than others?

(iv) Language

One of the problems in studying politics, whether they be domestic or world politics, is that everyone is familiar with this field. It is part of the day-by-day life of each person. The result is that there is a common, but imprecise, vocabulary. The same word, for example, 'nationalism', is used to describe aggressive behaviour, as well as loyalty behaviour. In practice, the analysis of world society is very much concerned with clarification of terms and concepts which are in general use, and with attempts to give precise meaning to them. The introduction of 'jargon' is merely part of the process by which language is enriched and by which there can be communication between persons with less misunderstanding. What is now regarded as ordinary usage, for example, 'power vacuums', and 'balance of power', was once regarded as 'jargon' just as 'cybernetic' and 'legitimized role behaviour' are now. Language is similar to perception: any imprecision leads to false observations.

It will be recalled that we commenced this discussion by examining the meaning of the terms 'international relations' and 'world society'. Just by asking ourselves what 'international' meant we were led to observe that there were features in world society other than national and state ones. Thinking about terms, examining our concepts, is an important part of analysis: we can come to different policy conclusions just by examining our own thinking processes.

The following discussion of terms and concepts is not intended to produce a clarification of meanings. This would require a much longer exposition. It is to make us aware of the need to be precise about the use of terms, and if necessary to explain special uses. There is a very long list of terms and concepts which are freely used in the scholarly literature and which may not be familiar to the general reader. These are usually explained by the writer. What we are concerned with now are examples of terms and concepts which are popularly used and which are used very loosely.

There was probably no more widely-used term in the literature dealing with International Relations than *'power'*. The earlier literature dealt almost exclusively with relations between 'powers' and with the relative power that states had. World society was thought to be governed by 'power politics'. While we are clearly aware that some states are more 'powerful' than others in a military, or economic or some other particular sense, it is still not clear what 'power' means.

Some writers have endeavoured to give a little more meaning to this concept by treating power as a way of describing the exercise of influence by one state on another along a spectrum commencing with ordinary arguments and persuasion through economic or diplomatic pressures to the final use of military force. Far from clarifying the concept, this merely demonstrates how unuseful it is. The 'power' of a state cannot be measured. How would one equate x number of battleships with y number of aeroplanes, or x number of forces with y economic strength, or x volume of trade with y ability to argue at a UN forum? Was the National Liberation Front in Vietnam more or less 'powerful' than the United States? As a consequence, this word which was once probably among the most used is now less frequently to be found in contemporary scholarly writings and when used it tends to signify power derived from legitimized authority.

In the minds of men it seemed that some states were not only more powerful than others, implying that there was some means of measuring relative power, but there could be a *balance of power*. Historians assert that it was the policy of some European governments to enter alliances so as to maintain the balance of power. As power cannot readily be quantified, it is difficult to see on what basis decisions were made. Furthermore, as has been pointed out by those who have discussed this concept,[20] it was never clear whether balance of power meant merely a balance, or a favourable balance, and it was highly unlikely that any state would sacrifice all its traditional, cultural and commercial links with other states in order to give first priority to maintaining a balance.

The terms *nation* and *state* have been used interchangeably. The League of Nations and the United Nations were descriptions of collective security organizations comprising states. The recognized term 'international relations' is really concerned with inter-state relations. This may seem a finicky point to make, but national groups within states have an important influence on events, and the term 'nation' should be reserved for such groups. There are such things as nationalities which are perhaps not quite the same thing as ethnic groups. Similarly, the term 'nationalism' is used to describe aggressive behaviour, loyalty to the state, independence movements, and a large number of different phenomena. Unless we are clear what we mean, our ideas and policies will be distorted: in Asia 'nationalist movements' were opposed by Western states immediately after the last war, and sometimes seen to be 'pro-communist'. They could have been seen as integrative and tending to create political stability in the longer term.

The study of world society is very much concerned with the study of *conflict*. However, the term 'conflict' itself always needs clarification according to the use to which it is put. The agricultural worker within a feudal system may have a happy relationship with his feudal lord. From a structural point of view the relationship is one of conflict and in certain circumstances this conflict could come to the surface and lead to violence. Or is conflict to be reserved for overt conflict, the evidence of which would be hostile behaviour? Sometimes conflict is used to mean violence. Some elements of conflicts are perhaps present in all social systems, as they are in the economic system where choice must be made as to alternative uses of resources. This is yet another meaning, and competition is another. Some conflict is an essential and beneficial process, yet the same term is used to describe processes which are destructive to everyone concerned.

Philosophers and sociologists have used the word *authority* and discussed it at length over many hundreds of years, and it is part of everyday language. The one term is used to describe the status of governments whether they derive their authority from acceptable electoral procedures or from the use of coercive force. Authority can be used to indicate professional knowledge. Is the 'authority' of a mediator derived from the United Nations which appointed him, from coercive power he can rely upon, from his own personal attributes, or from the acceptance of the parties concerned with this role as mediator? Are these sources of the same kind of authority?

Nonalignment, neutralism, neutrality, are all terms which need to be used carefully but which sometimes are used interchangeably. When Mr Dulles spoke of the 'immorality' of nonalignment, he apparently was mistaking nonalignment for neutrality, for he could not understand how anyone could be neutral in the conflict which he perceived between American and Soviet values and institutions. Nonaligned states are not 'neutral'; they speak their minds freely on any issue, sometimes criticizing one state, sometimes another.

It has never been clear what constitutes *aggression* and lawyers have not been able to agree. The term is used in the United Nations Charter as is also the concept of defence against aggression. In the context aggression seems to be the use of violence in attempting to change existing structures, whereas defence of existing structures by alliances and threats seems not to be aggressive. In the same way there is confusion about the notion of *intervention*. When country *A* appears to be giving assistance to some minority within country *B* this is intervention with aggressive intent, whereas when country *A* gives assistance to the government of country *B* when it is under internal threat this is 'lawful intervention'. Furthermore, non-intervention such as withdrawal of military supplies after conflict has occurred is in effect intervention.

There are some terms that are found to be useful in a particular subject, though they may not be in common use. In the theatre people enact *'roles'*. They must deliberately act a part and not behave as they would in their own life. Each of us enacts 'roles' – as a student, a member of a family or a fullback. It is convenient to talk of *'role behaviour'* in political analysis to draw a distinction between the influence of the personality of a leader and the influence of the role on him.

One could go on with terms of this nature, such as deterrence, self-defence, and others. In addition to these descriptive terms and concepts there are many methodological ones which need clarification and precise use, such as hypothesis, theory, probability, and others.

Experience is that one's thinking alters and one's conclusions change as the direct consequence of precision in the use of terminology. It is an important part of the analysis itself to obtain clarity of the phenomena being analysed, and if possible to find what are called *'operational definitions'*, that is, the precise measure that could be applied to the concept. What is democracy? It can be described as government for and by the people, but this does not say much in terms of alternative institutions. The Soviet or the United States systems can be regarded as no less or more democratic than each other. What do we mean by *participation*? If, however, we can translate these terms into operational definitions, then they are given a precise meaning. Legitimization of authority could conceivably be measured by the number of political prisoners or persons held under restraint, by the degree of press censorship, by the amount of control exercised over education. There may be many other operational definitions, and perhaps all of them together are relevant.

Precision is required not merely to ensure logical thought, but also to enable communication both in writing and verbally among those who are concerned with the study of a particular phenomenon. Experience is that scholars working together even within the same discipline take two or three years to learn a common language, and a good deal of time is consumed in conference discussions in clarifying what is being said. Communication across disciplines is especially difficult because the same words are often used and given wholly different meanings. 'Behaviouralism' in Psychology refers to the work of one particular psychologist who had a theory about reflex actions. 'Behavioural' in International Relations means interdisciplinary and scientific.

Language is not only the means by which we communicate ideas. It also helps to perpetuate them, even though they can be shown to be fallacious. Think of all the expressions we use that imply some theory or explanation of life. When we do not understand fully why things happen as they do, why we have a run of happy events followed by a run of sad ones, we search for an explanation. Laws of chance are not very satisfactory as explanations of a run of bad luck. Nor do we believe that we might have noticed only those events which were happy or sad because we were in a mood to be happy or sad. Failing to find an explanation, we settle for an explanation like 'the wheel of fortune', or 'the swing of the pendulum'. We relate our experience to something we know and do understand. This is using an analogy: we are saying, our experience is like the turning of a wheel or the movements of a pendulum. Sometimes analogies are good ones, and do help explain. Often they are poor ones and are misleading. Those who have studied world society have used many analogies, and sometimes they have seemed to be satisfactory because they have not been examined sufficiently carefully. We still speak of 'power balances', 'power vacuums'. When Britain decided to pull out of South East Asia and the Persian Gulf some people expected another great power to move in because of the 'vacuum' left, implying that the people in the region counted for nothing. Increases in national defences are sometimes justified by a need to restore a power balance. When we think about these terms and phrases we soon realize that they do not tell us much about world society.

We can easily become slaves to words, whereas words are meant to be used as tools of thought or as means of conveying some idea. This is why we have to invent new words from time to time to represent some new idea which cannot be represented by existing words. We have been referring to 'perceived relationships' instead of just 'relationships'. When one stops to think, it is apparent that all relationships are perceived, but we do not always stop to think and sometimes it is necessary to use a new term just to bring some feature to attention. Most politicians refer to *'national interest'* and justify their policies in terms of what they say is 'national interest'. But what does this term mean? There are very many competing and conflicting interests in every community, and what is in the interest of one group may be harmful to another. Is 'national interest' that which history later proves to be beneficial, or is it just what politicians believe it is? It is not a very useful term because it cannot be given a precise meaning. What do we mean by independence, loyalty, a common culture? We cannot say exactly; but we have, nevertheless, a vague idea of what is meant, and these vague ideas control our thinking and judgement in particular situations.

The dangers of vague thinking are very great. Indeed, false perceptions, false images and vague thinking create many situations of conflict. Take balance of power once again. What is usually meant is a favourable balance: we must be in a stronger position than the likely enemy. We ourselves are not aggressive, but we must increase our defences to restore a 'balance'. The likely enemy does the same thing. Before long there is an arms race. Our policies have become self-prophesying and self-defeating. We prophesied that the other state was a likely enemy, and our actions led him to respond in a way that made him an enemy. We also defeated the purpose of our defences by stimulating an arms race. As another example, take the idea of aggressiveness. We are not aggressive, but there is a possibility (we believe) that others are different from us and are likely to be aggressive. We, therefore, take steps to defend ourselves. Others think in the same way. Our defences are evidence of aggressiveness, as are their defences. The assumption of aggressiveness inevitably leads to conditions which support the assumption. Perhaps if it had been assumed that others behaved as we do and were not aggressive, and if they had acted on the same assumption, there could have been conditions of friendship created that justified this assumption.

Our thinking leads us to invent words, but language also influences our thinking. Words are, after all, only symbols. If we use one symbol to describe one kind of behaviour, and the same symbol to describe different behaviour, we will tend to regard the two different behaviours as having something in common. In describing states and world society we tend to use the same language as was developed to describe social situations. Is 'aggression' in animals the same as 'aggression' among states? Even different phenomena in world society are sometimes given the one symbol. Is the 'nationalism' of new states the same as the 'nationalism' of Hitler's Germany? It is necessary to question the use of terms – these symbols – to make sure that we are not being misled in our thinking by an inadequate set of symbols. We must also be prepared to invent new symbols where they are required.

(v) Mirror images and stereotypes

One of the consequences of the universal habit of thinking that it is others who are likely to be untrustworthy, deceitful and aggressive, is that each nation has exactly the same view of others, and exactly the same view of itself. All nations think others are likely to be aggressive, and all think that they themselves are peace-loving and more trustworthy than others. Scholars who have studied conflicts find that parties to any one conflict have the same view of each other, say the same kind of things about each other, and attribute the same kind of motives to each other. This, for obvious reasons, is called the 'mirror image'. In fact, the parties to one dispute say the same kind of things about each other as do the different parties involved in other disputes. The same mirror image is present when people and groups are antagonistic, as can readily be shown by asking them to write down answers to a series of questions asking what they think of each other.

We usually have fixed images of others: shopkeepers, university professors and school teachers, Chinese, Japanese, Americans, communists, fascists, spinsters, bachelors, mothers-in-law. This is what is called a 'stereotype'. A stereotype is a cast or mould used in printing, but it has now also this meaning of a fixed mental impression. We expect people to match our image of them – and because we expect them to do so we mainly observe those features which fit the impression. Americans and Russians, Indians and Pakistanis, Arabs and Israelis have mirror images of one another of hostility and untrustworthiness, and these images are stereotypes into which every American, every Russian, every Indian, Pakistani, Arab and Israeli must fit – except, of course, those few one might happen to get to know rather well. These are then special cases!

The question arises, why do we make assumptions of aggressiveness in the first place, and have these mirror images and stereotypes? If human instincts of aggressiveness are not necessarily the fundamental causes of conflicts in world society, if it is false perceptions, prejudices and acquired habits of observation that lead to conflict, where do they originate? Why do we not have favourable images, and flattering stereotypes that would lead to behaviour that encouraged peaceful and cooperative relationships?

There are many features of our psychological make-up which distort our thinking and observations. Some people do, in fact, tend to have favourable images of others. More frequently this is not so. For reasons of personal security we need to identify with others, that is we need to feel we have something in common with others and that we can share our experiences, and face problems with the support of others. We identify first with a family unit, then perhaps with a school class, and step by step with wider groups. Only a few people are able to identify with the human race; the more usual limit is with a linguistic, religious or racial group. This identification with others is a defence against the unknown. It is a desirable quality socially because it leads to cohesion, to community relationships and group solidarity. The interests of the group can in this way be more important to the individual than his own personal interests. But the wider consequences of identification are to restrict relations with outside groups, and to provide a source of antagonisms which otherwise might not exist. Tribalism, and various forms of nationalism, are, at least in part, a consequence of this need of persons to belong to a group and to preserve the group as a separate social unit. One of the great problems of Africa today is that little thought was given by European colonists to tribal and national units. Boundaries were drawn which cut across ethnic boundaries. The governments which have taken over from the colonial administrations seek to maintain the old boundaries for fear of loss of status or territorial control, and this leads sometimes to conflict within some of the new states as each national group endeavours to win back its identity and to gain the security that identity is felt to give.

It is most difficult if not impossible to force different national groups into the one social and political unit. However, given the separate identity of groups, they are usually happy to cooperate extensively with others. They demand the opportunity to decide whether, to what extent and in what form to cooperate. International institutions and federations emerge. Perhaps we must have a lot more separate nations and states before we can arrive at a world society in which there is close cooperation between nations and states, and a well-organized world community.

What we are now observing in world society is not merely the demand of peoples to be free of foreign rule, but to be free also of overlords of all kinds, whether they be indigenous landowners taking an unfair proportion of the returns of the land, or members of other ethnic groups that are in a dominating administrative or financial position. There is a struggle going on everywhere for identity, and it is accompanied by attempts to gain participation in all decisions that affect the individual. It is a struggle for equality of opportunity, for self-respect which cannot be present when there is racial prejudice, and for means of expression in addition to the formal processes of voting and electing representatives to parliaments. This drive for identity and participation has led to many social revolutions in the past. It is more apparent in world society today than ever before just by reason of the fact that it is now universal. It also affects relationships between great powers, some of which encourage, and some of which discourage, the social and political changes that are occurring within other states.

There are all manner of other influences that control our thinking and observations about world society: the level of education, the degree of fear and stress that we are experiencing, the political institutions that control our behaviour and the nature of the mass media. World society is the most complex of all human organizations, being the most extensive of them all. It is difficult enough to predict the behaviour of individuals whom we know well, and to adjust to them. Prediction of the behaviour of states and units within world society is seemingly impossible. We can be forgiven for relying upon our prejudices, and for acting on false information and distorted perceptions. We can never know all the facts, let alone predict the future behaviour of states and peoples. Later we will turn to consider how governments, which comprise persons with prejudices and distorted images, can conduct policies that will achieve their aims.

(vi) Models and approaches
In addition to perceptions of others, we all tend to have images or concepts of world society that influence our judgements of events. The 'billiard ball' and other models have already been mentioned. Important differences in policy occur because of differences in images or models of world society. Some scholars and politicians hold the view that conflicts are best settled by great powers pressing some agreement upon parties, while others take the view that the parties themselves must determine their own relationships. This is because some have an image of world society in which relations are based on power, some on laws, and some on more complex influences. These

images and models become even more influential when people consider them as indicating what 'ought' to be done, and not merely what
'is'. If our image of world society were one comprising states, then
state policy might reasonably be directed to giving assistance to other
states threatened with internal secession movements. But if our image
of world society were one of linkages, especially linkages among
similar cultural and language groups in different states, then state
policy might reasonably be directed to giving assistance to elements
within states that wished to be independent or to join with other
similar groups in other states. Our models or images enter into all our
thinking. The important thing is to be aware of them so that we can
examine them and test them against reality.

6. *Self-defeating strategies*

We have looked at problems of perception, including images of world society. Our perceptions and images can be shown sometimes to be impossible. They are, typically, antagonistic and reflect suspicion and fear, even though the evidence advanced to justify such perceptions does not stand up to examination. There appear to be two influences at work, some basic element in relations between authorities that makes them suspicious of each other, and, perhaps arising out of this, assumptions and perceptions of the aggressiveness and deceit of others.

It is possible to explain the basic element of suspicion and fear of others in biological and in psychological terms, for example, the fear of the unknown, dislike of habits and customs that are foreign, a biological urge to identify with one's own ethnic groups and to be correspondingly hostile towards others. These responses could, however, be the outcome of environmental conditions. They need not necessarily be an inherent part of the organism. It is important that we should know whether hostility is an inevitable human trait, or a result of perceived conditions. If the first, then peaceful relations will require some third party control and coercion – which does not seem possible. If the second, then different sets of remedies suggest themselves, especially more knowledge about decision making processes and the avoidance of behaviour that is perceived as aggressive.

(i) Social exchange and the differentiation of power
A sociologist has traced the way in which ordinary social exchange can leave one party to a transaction in the debt of another, and thus establish a chain of interactions that could lead to hostility and defensive postures.[21] Most social exchange is reciprocal. You say 'how do you do' and your friend says 'how do you do'. You entertain and you are entertained back. You go out to dinner and take a present. In Asia the gift ritual is highly developed – and sometimes

79

mistaken for bribery by those not familiar with it. But there are occasions on which the exchange is not reciprocated, and one party remains in the debt of the other. One party may not have the resources necessary for reciprocity, or may have ample goods and services available but not ones that are highly valued by the other. Clearly an exchange between two parties, one of which has goods and services more highly valued than those of the other, will be in the favour of the former. He will be able to exact a favourable exchange rate, and ultimately he will be in a 'powerful' position, that is, a postion in which he can influence the behaviour of the other. In due course he might be able to acquire some of the resources of the less favoured party to compensate for the debt, or gain some special privileges at the expense of this party.

Thus, out of ordinary social exchange there can arise a differentiation of power. If one wants to be 'independent' and not under the 'power' of another, or if one wishes to dominate another, then one needs to be in the position (a) of possessing all essential goods and services, (b) of having several alternative sources for these so as not to be dependent on any one party, (c) of having an ability to take by force if necessary any goods and services that are vital, and (d) of being able to live without the goods and services possessed by others. Applying sanctions against a country is an example of exercising this type of power over it. By examining these four conditions it can be determined whether the application of sanctions against a country can be effective.

In this perspective it is easy to surmise how tribes and city states viewed each other, and especially those that were conscious of being subject to coercion or blackmail by others. Each social unit must almost inevitably be conscious of the desirability of being independent of others, despite inequalities of needs and resources. The fact that one of the four means of maintaining independence is to use force in securing essential needs makes even more favourably placed groups feel insecure, and the danger of losing independence to more favourably placed groups makes others feel insecure. All feel that there is a need for some measure of self-defence or self-protection in some form. A first measure of self-defence is to define territory by defining boundaries, and once these are defined they require protection.

There are all manner of factors that increase this social exchange problem. Change, for example, new inventions, discoveries of minerals, exploration of new territories and new sources of supply, changes in ideologies, all alter one or another of the four main elements in a 'social exchange'. They therefore alter the relative power positions or levels of independence of each party. In one century Britain is in a strong bargaining postion, in another Japan. If one party is exploring and acquiring new territories, the other feels it must try to do the same. If one introduces some new form of defence, the other feels it must. Whether the relationships are between primitive societies or between modern states, the same processes of social exchange occur, and change tends to increase defensive behaviour.

We have here a real situation of competition, inequality and differentiation of power – just through accidents of resources, distribution and skills, and the relative value of goods and services being exchanged. One does not have to postulate human aggressiveness. Identification with an ethnic or tribal group, hostility to the foreign or neighbouring tribe, the perception of aggression and fear, can be an outcome of social evolution and social exchange. They may or may not be inherent in human psychology or biology: there is in social exchange a sufficient explanation of social interaction.

At this point, however, perception plays a role. The party less endowed with vital resources, in a less advantageous exchange position, suffers a sense of injustice. 'Values' attached to equality of opportunity and independence are being destroyed. The rich are getting richer and the poor poorer – and there seems no way out. The privileged will wish to maintain existing relations, and the poor will wish to upset them – each using violence if necessary. This can be imagined in primitive relationships, and it is also a very real element in contemporary state relationships. The underdeveloped countries of today feel prejudiced and threatened, becoming relatively poorer and poorer as time goes on, and as exchange relations become less favourable to them. Important 'values' are at stake: they feel they should have better opportunities to compete, more control over the exploitation of their resources, improved terms of trade. They look upon the world situation and their position in it from a background of exploitation – their lands and resources were taken in the past by white settlers because they did not have bargaining power, techniques, and all the requirements of independence. There has been 'aggression', and it now continues in another form because of unfavourable terms of trade or rates of exchange.

Once this differentiation of power has occurred, there can be one of two responses. The less privileged party may adapt to the adverse conditions and accept a role determined by others, as did colonial peoples and as did the agrarian worker under feudal conditions. The different castes in India seemed to accept their relative social positions and inequality of privileges. The individual and small group is adaptable, and psychologists and sociologists have tended to emphasize this ability to adapt, at least once really basic physiological needs are satisfied. This process of adaptation is known as 'socialization', or integration of the person or group within the environment by processes of adjustment. On the other hand, the response could be an endeavour to change the environment and to redress the imbalance in social relations. Political scientists tend to question the belief of psychologists and sociologists that people are so malleable and willing to adjust to a hostile environment. They argue that there are human values other than basic physiological ones, and that if these are not satisfied there will be psychological or physiological disturbances. Frustration and the use of violence can result. This is probably a more realistic emphasis in modern conditions in which peoples are aware of opportunities. Being aware of alternatives probably lessens willingness to adapt. The feudal worker in Asia now knows that there are other economic systems, and colonial peoples know that they can achieve freedom. The developing states are now struggling to redress the trade balance by activities in the United Nations Conference on Trade and Development. Increased expectations probably further decrease willingness to sublimate desires and to adjust to the circumstances of the environment. One can expect that those whose privileged position are threatened no less look around for means of defending themselves against demands for change.

These two responses, adjustment to the environment, and attempts to alter the environment, are not confined to the relations between groups and nations amongst which there has been a differentiation of power. What we have been discussing is a general behavioural pattern of response which occurs at all social and political levels. Within each group the same process operates. Leaders and factions find it necessary to protect their positions against popular demand for change. They could do this by adapting their behaviour to the requirements of the political environment and by changing their policies. More usually they endeavour to fight off political opposition by propaganda or even by repression. It is important to note that the same consequences of differentiation of power occur *within* political groups as occur *among them*. We will find that a major origin of conflict between groups is to be found in conflict *within* them. A privileged leader who needs support to defend his position, or an underprivileged group that perceives itself as being suppressed by leadership, often looks outside the territories of the group for support. If support is forthcoming there is thus a spill-over of internal conflict into world society.

Let us, then, trace through the consequences of this 'real' situation of conflict that results from social exchange and differentiation of power and from the 'perception' of aggressiveness that less favoured people have of those threatening their independence. Let us trace through the measures that are taken by each either to protect existing positions against change or to force change.

In the relations among states these measures have included isolation, independent national (or tribal) defence, alliances, balance of power, regional collective security, communal collective security, thermonuclear deterrence, and nonalignment. As each failed to achieve its purpose the next was introduced. There is, therefore, a time sequence. However, it should be noted that, as with all cases of evolutionary trends, there are no discontinuities. One phase merges into the next. Furthermore, no new phase totally eliminates past ones: collective security did not eliminate national defence. But it is convenient to discuss each, to see why each failed, and why other forms emerged.

(ii) Isolation

Withdrawal or isolation is a common defence mechanism in individuals, and it also occurs in the behaviour of groups, especially when there is a perceived external threat. At primitive political levels, where there is little industrialization and interdependence, isolation in some degree was probably the most frequent reaction to external threat. This applies to the privileged no less than to the underprivileged. Even powerful states like the Soviet Union, China and the United States have all experienced withdrawal in some form in an attempt to protect themselves against external influences. The position of states that are relatively satisfied with international society is stronger than those who wish to change it, but both perceive a need to preserve what they have, and to effect whatever changes appear to be in their interests. The act of military self-defence is in itself an act of isolation, or, more precisely, a reaction against conditions in which an effective isolation is impossible.

Political and strategic isolation implies a degree of cultural and commercial isolation. These forms of isolation are a common response to adverse internal and environmental conditions. Germany's 'autarky' of the thirties was a response to widespread unemployment internally, and an absence of marketing opportunities externally. In due course there was a strategic policy that increased isolation. It is difficult to determine which occurred first, the commercial or the political and strategic withdrawal. Once protectionism was pursued as a means of solving internal economic problems, and especially once it was accompanied by a build-up of forces, political withdrawal was bound to follow – with all kinds of unforeseen military consequences.

At a very early stage in social organization self-defence by walls and armed forces was seen to be the appropriate means of isolation from undesired influences, while still permitting those that were seen to be an advantage. Self-defence is calculated to obtain the best of both worlds: interdependence yet isolation from any undesired influences. While some measure of withdrawal is always possible, 'isolation', meaning total withdrawal, is not a response that can be followed effectively in a world of interdependent peoples.

(iii) National self-defence
Defence forces have been so widely associated with independent states that they have become a symbol of statehood. 'Power' has been equated with the size of forces. The origins of national defence forces are not clear. In many cases they seem to have arisen out of amalgamations of private armies. They can be traced back to feudal or city-state conditions in which sovereign regions within national groupings existed. From earliest times their role was internal as well as external defence, and it may be that the internal defence aspect was the more important in many cases. Certainly this would have been the case whenever economic and social structures could be maintained only through coercion. This was probably the case in Britain in feudal periods and in some early stages of industrialization, when 'social exchange' divided sharply privileged from under-privileged.

However effective national defences may have been for internal law and order, they have proved self-defeating against external threats. In a world society of independent political units, each fearful of the influence of the other, each suspicious of the 'aggressiveness' of the other, defence forces by one nation are perceived as a threat to others, leading to defensive responses by them. These are seen as evidence of a hostile intent, thus giving rise to increased defence forces by the one nation that originally perceived a threat – and so on. This 'escalation' of defence forces tends to create conditions of fear and threat, and increased insecurity. Forces, introduced to increase security, have thus defeated their purposes.

(iv) Alliances

Alliances or agreements for mutual self-defence are known among tribes, and they have always been a usual feature of relations between states. Peoples with common interests to pursue or defend are likely to cooperate, and it is not surprising that peoples of the same ethnic, language or cultural groups come together. The inadequacy of national defences leads nations to seek mutual assistance agreements.

As is the case with national defences, alliances are for purposes of internal security in many instances. A government that does not have popular support sometimes seeks external assistance to combat 'subversion'. Subversion can usually be attributed to a foreign power and made to appear as though it were an external threat. Some of the governments of Asia sought security from internal threat by membership of SEATO. Some of the governments of Europe rely upon NATO or the Warsaw Pact for internal security.

The greater powers have an interest in ensuring that there is no political change in smaller states within their spheres of influence, and alliance structures give them the opportunity to intervene. Alliances seem to be strongest between large and small states that have these interacting internal and strategic interests. They aim to preserve existing political and social structures, and in a world society of communist and capitalist states, alliance structures have this functional role.[22]

(v) Power balances

Alliances have a balancing effect in a world society that includes two major powers with different and opposing ideologies. However, balance of power has a special meaning. By it is intended to convey a continuing policy by which one state throws its weight behind one state or group of states at one time, and another at another, to maintain a power balance. It was the policy Britain was said to have followed in Europe. Whether Britain and other states followed such a policy deliberately, or whether it just happened for other reasons to suit the interests of the power at the time to alter relationships, is an open question.[23] There is a tendency to confuse the presence or otherwise of a balance, with a deliberate policy of balancing. There is today a thermonuclear 'balance', but there is no deliberate policy by Britain, China or any other state to act as balancer between the two thermonuclear powers.

The whole notion of balance is an unsatisfactory one, as we have already seen. It is not clear whether by 'balance' is meant a favourable balance, or imbalance, or equilibrium. Furthermore, such a policy would require a government to give its policy of balancing priority over all other considerations – even traditional cultural links and trading interests. One scholar has dealt fully with these criticisms.[24] As is the case with alliances, the purpose of balancing would be to prevent change: war, or a deliberate breaking of the rules of balancing would be the only means of making some fundamental change in power relations.

(vi) Collective security

Collective security was seen to be the way of avoiding these problems associated with national defences, alliances and balance of power. There has been in the minds of men the belief that there would or could be a gradual extension of social control, including law and order, from the smallest unit, that is, the family or the family tribe, to the state. It was observed by early philosophers that conflict within the tribe was eliminated by tribal leadership and law, and sub-sequently inter-tribal conflict was eliminated by the creation of the state. It would appear logical to assume that this associative process would continue until a world order were established in which conflict between states would be eliminated. Indeed, this seems to have been the basis of classical Western thinking. The idea of an extending world order has appeal even in modern times; the concept of 'one world' or of 'world government' as a means of avoiding war rests upon it.

If such a world order were possible, it would be logical to argue that those enforcement procedures that ensure peace within a municipal community could be developed within the world community. However, there are both logical and practical reasons for rejecting this evolutionary theory. The reason for the integration of tribes was not merely to enforce inter-tribal peace, but equally to afford protection of tribes against attack. The expectation of the development of a world order would be logical only if the world were under attack from another planet. There are, furthermore, practical reasons for regarding world government as unreal. There is basic discontinuity between the growth of the state and the further extension of authority to embrace the world. First, cultural and geographic differences, differences in natural resources, differences in political institutions and customs, and other differences among states make any continuity in the process quite unreal. Problems of decentralization in the world arena are different in kind from those in the local environment. At what point the discontinuity occurs, at what size a social unit must be regarded as no longer subject to the techniques and forces operating in a community, may be a question for argument; but that there is a point at which unification is not possible is apparent in the modern world.

Secondly the problems of conquest and of maintenance of law and order by a central authority are quite different in a world community from those in a local state. Psychological and political responses and sentiments of nationalism, racialism, freedom, and independence at once enter into a world society in a way which is incompatible with central control and domination. In retrospect, it is no surprise that events showed Roman imperialism, as a practical military and political procedure, to be impossible of achievement and ultimately unstable even to the limited degree in which it was accomplished. The fate of subsequent imperialisms is likewise understandable. It is even more difficult to envisage how a world government would operate in modern times even though it were founded in the wake of a nuclear war, for, assuming the continued existence of organized society, social and economic units would in due course be capable of producing nuclear weapons which would place each of them on a basis of military equality with the central authority.

In academic circles and in the popular belief, there are few theories more generally held than that international organization and international control of sovereign states are logically an extension of the processes of national law and order. Quincy Wright asserts: 'The role of violence in international law is related to the role of violence in municipal law not only by analogy but also by homology and perhaps by identity.'[25] In subsequent chapters he deals with the special problems experienced in international law in terms which indicate that in his view they are problems of growth and evolution, and not difficulties arising out of incompatibility with national law.

Although widely held for many generations, however, the belief that national law will in due course evolve into international law is logically in error. The analogy between national and international law leads to very misleading speculation. To go further and to argue identity is an error based on the false assumption of the existence of some continuous process commencing with independent sovereign powers and ending in international law and order.

International law employs the same terms as national law; and it is in part this homology which has led to the assumption that the two have some common foundation, and that in due course international enforcement will develop. There is, however, no common foundation; there is no justification even for the use of the same terms. International law, so called, is a purely voluntary observation of codes. It is not law in any sense of the exercise of sovereign powers. In the national community, law enforcement is applied against a relatively few citizens who might have the desire to break a law. Almost none of these individuals has any final social responsibilities in community decision. They must submit. They have no rights with respect to law breaking. The rights of the individual to freedom of action are regarded by law makers as relatively unimportant compared with the general interests and welfare of the millions who make up the social unit. At best, certain 'moral' rights may in some cases be recognized, the exercise of which may lead to alterations in law. In international relations, on the other hand, there are no more than one hundred or so nations, each one of which is acting with full responsibility for its own final decisions and is prepared to defend them as being proper, justifiable, and necessary in the interests of its people. An analogy between two so totally different sets of circumstances is logically not justified.

Any enforcement of international 'law' that might take place is, therefore, enforcement by one or more nations on behalf of their own interests and against those of others. It may be that the enforcing group claims to be acting in the interests of the world community, the claim made by democratic government when enforcing law against the private citizen. Equally, the nations against whom enforcement action is taken can claim that they represent the interests of the world community. In practice, however, neither can represent or be regarded as representing 'world interests'. There is no entirely valid analogy with national law enforcement. The closest resemblance would be found in a national society undergoing political revolution, in which one party endeavours to impose its will upon all others.

There are many major differences between the organization of a state and that of an international system that makes analogy of little value. In a state there can be final control of government by the people, usually by election processes. In the international community there is no such control, save war, which it is the purpose of the organization to prevent. International enforcement is a form of tyranny and as such will never be accepted by states against which it is exercised. Again, the national police function has a deliberately deterring effect because it punishes specific crimes. There is no such motivation in international law. There are indeed such things as war crimes, and war trials. In the main, however, international force is used to preserve some interest or to frustrate some ambition, but not to punish on any basis of 'accepted law'. The 'wrongdoer' is that nation which loses in war; the crime is failure to win. The victor becomes the 'lawmaker'.

One practical objection to the theory of an expanding legal process relates specifically to the nuclear age. The problem is no longer one of merely reducing the frequency of war; it has become imperative to eliminate war of all kinds, for fear that even a limited war could result in the use of large nuclear weapons. Even if world government of sovereign states were eventually possible by peaceful means, the time required to achieve this end would rule it out as a practical procedure in modern conditions.

(vii) Disarmament and arms control

Erroneous views on the nature of social evolution, and the false expectation that there would be a relinquishment of sovereignty, led to policies and structures which could not even in theory achieve the results sought. National policies of defence were not effective in preventing war, nor in controlling change. The League of Nations did not develop toward world government, nor has the United Nations. At best, these traditional policies and structures have had a relevance in the sense that tribal warfare once had a relevance to social organization – the defence of national interests by force and through international alliances are stages through which world society has had to pass.

One response to this sequence of disappointments has been an endeavour to negotiate disarmament, or arms control. In the League days this was a failure, and it was again in the fifties when public opinion seemed to demand of governments some way out of the escalation of nuclear weapons, and the dangers inherent in this. It is unlikely that governments were ever serious about disarmament. Perceived conditions seemed to require national defences and alliances. The conditions still existed which originally had promoted defences, so there was little prospect of eliminating, or even of controlling them by international negotiation. Differentiated power, and perceptions of threat which provoked defences are not eliminated by disarmament.[26]

What is clear from this sequence of defence strategies is that in social relations an attitude tends to set in motion processes that justify the attitude. A friendly gesture invokes a friendly response, thus seeming to justify the friendly gesture. A hostile attitude creates hostility. There is a direct relationship between thinking and foreign policies of governments and world events. There developed after the Second World War a school of 'political realists' who argued that the facts of aggressiveness and power should be recognized, and that 'idealism' in the form of functional cooperation was misplaced. The 'proof' was war. What the 'political realists' failed to appreciate was that an assumption of aggressiveness, and the organization of world society into power blocs, would inevitably lead to defensive and aggressive responses that would lead to war. Nothing was 'proved' except that certain policies invoke certain responses. If the intentions of governments were security and peace, then their strategic policies were self-defeating – they brought about just those conditions they were intended to prevent.

7. *A modified view*

So far we have been concerned with two interacting influences in world society, and the policy consequences which flow from them. We saw the way in which people, individually and as groups, view themselves and each other, and the way in which prejudice, insecurity or lack of information can distort reality. This was our starting point in the study of world society on the grounds that all relationships are perceived relationships. 'Reality' is what we believe it to be. The behaviour of others is, effectively if not in reality, what we believe it to be. Our prejudices and misperceptions tend, for many psychological and perhaps biological reasons, to be malign and not benign – they tend to assume the worst of others, and to make us defensive of our own kith and kin.

Second, we saw the way in which social exchange ultimately leads to a differentiation of power, thus creating defensive and aggressive responses within any social organization, and especially among different national groups. These responses arise out of organizational conditions and not biological mechanisms. We have seen how societies can be aggressive by reason of environmental conditions only – there is no need to assume some built in human aggressiveness.

The predispositions to perceive inaccurately and in malign ways, and the hostility between groups that seems to be invited by social conditions, interact and feed on each other. The defensive mechanisms employed appear to confirm to all concerned the aggressive intent of others, and escalation of defence finally results in the insecurity of all. Attempts to transfer responsibility for peace and security in world society to a supra-national body are doomed to failure in a world system of independent and nuclear states. In any event, it is not possible to coerce peoples into behaving in ways unacceptable to them. Whether in domestic or world society, conforming behaviour can be brought about only by acceptable socialization, not by coercion.

We have already learned this in most small group relationships. It was once thought that relations between employer and employees in industry should and had to be within a hire-and-fire, or some direct coercive relationship. Conditions of work were not regarded as important in the relationship because labour was to management merely the extension of machinery. The arm of the worker was little different from the lever of a machine. Later conditions of work, such as the work environment, hours and wages, holidays, came to be something about which there could be negotiation. These are termed the 'hygiene' factors, that is, the conditions that management saw to be necessary for efficient production. Today attention is directed to other conditions – participation in decision-making, degrees of responsibility to match ability, status, interest in work, discretion in adopting new procedures, and others of this kind. Coercion in any form is coming to be seen as counterproductive. Management of the old type – still existing in some of the largest and technologically advanced industries – has to suffer costs of strikes and to pay high wages to compensate for a failure to satisfy these values. At another level, in past days the 'delinquent' was punished in order to set an example to others, and to persuade him to conform. More and more courts are now interested in environmental circumstances and ways in which he has been deprived in society of what he needs, just as workers are deprived of their need to express themselves in the work environment. Probation officers try to help delinquents adjust to society by trying to change the immediate environment, and to give opportunities for personality development. So in education, social work, marriage guidance, and other fields of social relationships.

We have seen that the defence mechanisms and behaviour of states fail to achieve peace and security. They have been self defeating, as were the defence mechanisms of employers and employees, and those of society when confronting delinquents. Have we anything to learn about world society and its management from our experience at individual and small group levels? Every practitioner, that is, foreign office official and responsible politician, knows that there are problems of misperception and difference of interest in relations between states. But having decided that some nations are more friendly or more hostile than others, they rest largely on defensive policies, including secret agreements, espionage, counter-espionage, alliances, and even thermonuclear threats. Are there other influences to which attention needs to be paid which would offer some prospect of policies being less self defeating?

In our analysis of world society we will not be considering 'oughts' and 'shoulds' or 'if onlys'. To say that all states 'should' obey some set of laws, or 'if only' behaviour were different in some particular respects, is not helpful either in understanding world society or in finding ways of controlling it. What we have to do is to look at world society more carefully, be more realistic, and search for influences we have previously missed and which are essential to our understanding of it. In industrial relations 'management consultants' are now far less concerned with environmental conditions of work when they are asked to explain why production levels are not as high as management thinks they should be, or why there are go-slows and strikes. They realize that the problem is a human one – boredom and frustration. A good agitation is quite a relief: it gives men a role, a status. No improvement in conditions could remove the boredom and frustration of the worker on a production line. Advisers now search for other factors, and are interested in values, motivations, and human behaviour generally. They might suggest automation to eliminate some jobs, or they might say there is no solution in a given set of circumstances, short of shorter working hours, and wages for routine jobs far higher than wages for skilled jobs. This is turning organization and our judgement about rewards on their heads. May we not have to think as radically about problems of world society?

(i) Integrative influences

The negative aspects of social exchange – the differentiation of power, perceptions of hostility and defensive responses – have been reflected in traditional theories of international politics that place their main emphasis on the relative power of states. Morgenthau seems to base his thinking on an assumption that human nature is aggressive and power seeking.[27] Schwarzenberger would probably not disagree with the possibility that there could be a differentiation of power through social processes.[28] Both, however, end at the same point: world society comprises states of different power, smaller states must react to the behaviour of greater ones, and, in short, world society is explicable in terms of power politics.

But world society is more complicated than this: there are other aspects of social exchange to be taken into account. While state policies are essentially defensive, they also seek cooperation. The integrative aspect of world society, behaviour which is not defensive, has not received as much attention in history books and in theoretical analysis as defensive aspects. They are less dramatic. They are, nonetheless, probably more important to states in their day-to-day dealings, and furthermore, it is these which are of most interest if the purpose of our study of world society is to see how it can be regulated in the interests of peaceful relationships.

It seems to be an empirical fact that peoples, whether in small or large groups, value their independence, and consequently the four conditions of independence that we have already noted will tend to guide their behaviour. People will endeavour to have goods and services they regard as being important to them under their own control, and also goods important to others so that they can exchange them to good advantage; failing this, or in any case, they will try to make sure there are alternative sources of supply of any goods and services they must acquire, so as not to be held at ransom by any one supplier; failing this, or in any case, they would like to have the military or other coercive means to obtain goods and services they need and which may be withheld by others; and failing this, or in any event, they would like to have an ideology, a nationalism or strong motivation that enabled them to do without even valuable goods and services rather than fall under the sway of another group and lose independence of action.

But what do we mean by independence? Clearly no group of peoples in the modern world favours an independence that necessitates isolation. By independence is meant freedom from coercion by others in respect of opportunities to develop, freedom to maintain a culture, and generally those freedoms that are associated with individuals and groups living within any community. The right to be consulted and to participate, and the avoidance of discrimination and exploitation are parts of this independence. We must not take these four requirements of independence as absolutes: no group wishes to have all essential goods and services under its control, to coerce others to supply everything wished, or wholly to do without foreign goods and services. This means that there are forms of dependence and interdependence that are acceptable, if not welcome. What are these, and to what extent do they modify the power and defence dominated picture of world society which has been traditionally accepted?

(ii) Advantages of specialization
Specialization and exchange are means of increasing productivity and of acquiring goods and services not otherwise available. No group of people, no state, however large, can be self-sufficient in all the

resources and skills required to satisfy needs and demands in contemporary times. But even though the resources of some enabled them to be self-sufficient, there would still be gains from specialization. Group *A*, privileged because of valuable natural resources, and capable of producing all goods and services better than group *B*, nevertheless benefits by concentrating on the production of the goods and services it produces most efficiently, allowing *B* to concentrate on the goods and services it can produce most efficiently, and exchanging goods and services with *B*. Under this system *B* is also better off, at least, in terms of quantities of goods and services available. This is known as the 'comparative costs' theory.[29]

If there were free mobility of capital and labour throughout world society the inequalities resulting from social exchange would gradually diminish, thereby reducing differentiation of power and perceived threat to independence. The free trade advocates of the past argued that peace and prosperity would be assured if these conditions prevailed. Maybe. The reality is that mobility is costly and in any event all peoples want to determine the composition of their own populations, all people seem to want the opportunity to choose between an agricultural and an industrial life, and wish to see themselves advance materially and culturally at a rate enjoyed by others. All people want these forms of 'independence'. Despite this reality, however, comparative costs exercise a strong influence in world society, and comparative cost theory focuses attention on world society as a whole, and social exchange within it, regardless of the obstacles created by state boundaries and relative international immobility of labour and capital. It points to the opportunities and possible opportunities that exist for cooperation and interdependence without threat to independence, just as there is social exchange within a state with little threat or loss of individual independence. Comparative cost theory demonstrates that social exchange does not necessarily lead to a differentiation of power, though frequently in practice it does.

(iii) Nonalignment

Not only must we modify the view that a differentiation of power is the outcome of social exchange, we must also modify the view that there is necessarily a perception of threat once power is differentiated. No doubt this was once so in times of exploration and occupation in which military power was used by states to acquire sources of raw materials. In contemporary conditions even the smallest and weakest of states can retain their independence. Many new states have demonstrated this by 'nonalignment'. Despite their economic weakness, they have refused to be controlled in their internal and external policies. To some extent they have been able to do this because of the rivalry of the two thermonuclear states, the Soviet Union and the United States of America. But their voting at the United Nations and independent behaviour seem to suggest that a differentiation of power does not necessarily result in perceptions of external threat to security and independence.

Nonalignment has been one of the responses of states to the failure of alliances and collective security, and unlike the others, it is not a defensive response. In practice a policy of nonalignment is frequently not practical because internal political struggles and demands for a change tend to lead new states into accepting external military aid. Their nonaligned status is thereby compromised. However, nonalignment offers us a useful model and theory as do comparative costs. As a model, a world society of independent states, none great enough to influence world society, and each capable of acting independently in its political judgement in order to maximize its achievements, is a useful analytical device. It draws attention to some aspects of world society which are less conspicuous but nevertheless no less significant, than defence and alliance behaviour.[30] In any pure form it is unrealistic. Yet it describes a form of behaviour which is an alternative to the defensive alliance behaviour traditionally thought to be inevitable in a world society of relatively powerful and relatively powerless states. Smaller states are aware of restraints to their development imposed by terms of trade that they believe to be 'unjust', and of the 'exploitation' of foreign investment; but a power response to these seems not to be relevant. International action such as the United Nations Conference on Trade and Development to redress terms of trade, and internal action to prevent the export of profits, are within their capabilities. By these means they can obtain some of the benefits of specialization, foreign investment and the technologies of the powerful states, without necessarily perceiving any threat to independence.

(iv) Integration
Clearly, then, if there is no perception of threat there may be only a limited or contingency defensive posture, and active cooperation with other states. From time to time, however, and in particular cases, the degree of perceived threat will alter. A boundary dispute, an altered

defence programme, a social or political change within a neighbouring state and other changes of this kind can be perceived as a threat.
At least there are likely to be minorities within a state that interpret
change in others as a threat, and play upon the deep fears of the
community. The 'communist' threat has been exploited in this way in
the United States, and the 'imperialist' threat in the Soviet Union. It is
probably perception that determines in each case and at any particular time where on the defensive–integrative spectrum relations are
seen to lie. We know, from empirical studies that as tension increases
perception of hostility increases, leading to defensive responses which
themselves are perceived as evidence of hostility. Even nonaligned
states are subject to perceptions of hostility – though, in point of fact,
there are few examples of conflict between states that declare themselves nonaligned.

A question which is relevant in any study of world society is
whether relationships among states are tending and will tend to move
along the spectrum, and in which direction. Will there be tendencies
towards increased defensive responses or increased integration? Or
are states moving towards increased independence in the supply of
political judgements and services, and yet towards increased integration economically?

It needs to be acknowledged that integration, in the sense of
interdependence and international cooperation, is not an end in itself.
Integration is sometimes a useful means to an end – improved welfare
and cultural attainments may be possible as a result of it. It is,
however, relevant only where internal political patterns are already
established. Integration does not solve problems of political and
economic development, it merely extends the possibilities of development for those who are in a position to integrate. The Common
Market cannot solve the agricultural or industrial problems of Western Europe. They must be solved within each state on some common
basis, thus making integration possible. Then integration can lead to
further advances.

This observation is particularly important in relation to less
developed countries. 'African Unity' is an ideology; but it is not a goal
that can be attained until within each political unit there has been
established the conditions for integration. For instance, there has to
be an authority that wins the support of the community, a habit of
voluntary compliance with the decisions of that authority, a limited
probability of enforcement against transgressors, means of resolving
the continuing conflicts between aims people have and the restraints

imposed on them by authorities, and processes whereby political priorities, the holders of offices and the structure of offices can be changed to meet altering conditions and requirements. In short, before there can be integration with others there must be political development, the ability to change goals, to adapt to altered environmental circumstances, and yet to maintain a degree of stability and continuity in administration. From time to time, and especially in periods of rapid change, political development is subject to fundamental discontinuities – revolutions occur, making integration with others impossible. In such circumstances there are likely to be extreme ideologies – that is, systems of belief that are not subject to correction even after experience with reality – which make integration even more difficult.

We have tended to look to the future in terms of more and more political integration. Some people have spoken of 'one world', meaning a universal organization of people sharing similar values and ideologies. This is probably a false image. The characteristic feature of the contemporary world is an increase in the demand for political services – education, health, industrial organization, communications, law and order and others. There is a persistent demand for local participation in political decisions which determine priorities in relation to these. In any event these services are probably provided most efficiently on a local basis. There are cultural, environmental and many local circumstances to which services need to be adopted. Furthermore, there do not seem to be any advantages in scale for such services: the police force can be fully efficient when it is regionalized, provided it can keep in touch with police forces elsewhere. Educational services required in developing areas are not necessarily the same as those required in developed areas. In other words, the size of political units will probably always be small, and common services are likely to develop over large areas only when these areas are so alike that they require the same services. Integration follows similar development – it cannot promote it. It is even undesirable if it is not relevant to the circumstances. Many would say the Common Market is undesirable for this reason.

This being the case, we need to question the 'African Unity' ideology, and in particular to question policies designed to maintain the unity of existing states in which large sections wish to break away. The cry of 'economic viability' is irrelevant. There can always be international commerce. The real issue is 'political viability', and it may be that smaller and not larger units than we have today are desirable.

There are now more than twice as many independent states as there were before the last war. If one were to accept a power theory of world society, one would expect there to be less, and not more states, and less, not more independence. Empires have crumbled, and even spheres of influence are under constant threat as states within them seek increased freedom to follow their own internal and external policies. There are good reasons for believing there will be still more states created; the Biafran struggle is not the last of such struggles. Even greater powers such as Britain and India – and who knows, the Soviet Union and the United States – could evolve into looser federations. Demands for participation in issues of local concern, the administrative need to decentralize, and drives to preserve some aspects of separate cultures, are all influences that restrain the free exercise of power by greater states. Looking ahead, world society could readily move rapidly in the direction of smaller and smaller political units, local government units with extensive responsibilities, within economic units of increasing size.

There are some psychological and empirical reasons for suspecting that integration must rest on independence. It is difficult to impose cooperation even on those who would benefit from it; but voluntary integration can be effective. The history of the British Commonwealth lends support to this view. If Biafra had been allowed to break away at an early stage, a high degree of voluntary cooperation and integration with the rest of Nigeria might have resulted without the terrible costs that occurred. In any event an enforced integration creates trouble for the future. This is something to be taken into account in thinking about the future of East and West Germany, North and South Korea, North and South Vietnam and other such situations.

(v) Functional institutions

Independent political units find it possible to cooperate with others, even ones that have different cultures and ideologies. It is in the common interests of states to cooperate in the provision of some services that are needed across cultures and in all environments. Disease knows no political boundaries, and the activities of the World Health Organization, and other agencies of the United Nations provide a service to all states. The major technological contributions probably come from the economically and militarily powerful states, but the supply of technology through an international institution does not threaten the independence of even the smallest state. There is now a complicated network of international organizations, governmental and non-governmental, that supply services to most, and in some cases all states, regardless of size and status. The operations and political consequences of functional institutions have occupied the attention of scholars who have developed an interesting theory of 'functionalism', suggesting that it will be by this means that problems of power relations will finally be resolved.[31]

The activities of international corporations are commencing to inject into relations between states an influence which reduces the consequence of differentiated power. International corporations are at present centred within economically powerful states, but this is altering. The purpose of a corporation is to make profits, and management attempts to limit dividends and to avoid taxation, and to reinvest in order to make more profits. They are fast becoming public utilities or international institutions that render a service to states not otherwise in a position to develop resources. They are similar, in this respect, to intergovernmental functional institutions. International registration of international corporations, themselves comprising international corporations, are likely to develop and to operate with the encouragement and cooperation of developing states and on terms acceptable to them.

The four requirements of independence, outside the need for 'coercion', are becoming easier to satisfy in the contemporary world. Basic resources are more widespread. Oil and sources of power are available in most countries and with nuclear energy will be even more readily available in the future. Substitute materials such as plastics are readily produced. Rhodesia has demonstrated that one effect of sanctions has been the stimulation of local production. Furthermore, there has been an increase in alternative sources of supply so that in few cases are states likely to be deprived of their requirements. Even ideological differences and 'non-recognition' does not prevent states obtaining their essential requirements, as renewed contracts for the sale of wheat from Western countries to China demonstrate. The role of authorities is more and more to promote transactions, and less and less to preserve existing structures internally. We do seem to be moving toward a phase in international relations in which integrative trends may be more influential than defensive ones. These can be encouraged – just as defensive ones have been promoted in the past. States are not just in competition with each other for scarce resources – they have also a self-interest in integrative behaviour. The more defensive the behaviour of one state, the more defensive is the behaviour of others. The more integrative, the more integrative is the behaviour of others. Perhaps civilization will in due course be rescued from its defensive and self-destructive postures by technological developments and the need for functional cooperation which tends to impose integration despite ourselves.

(vi) The reality of authority
Having canvassed defensive postures and integrative influences, we must acknowledge the reality of authority, and the drive of authorities to preserve themselves. If all governments represented the interests of those over whom they exercise authority, it could be assumed that each would enter into universal functional arrangements where these seemed to lead to greater efficiency in producing goods, services and cultural values required. But this is not the case. Authorities are frequently acting in the interests of minorities or majorities, and frequently defending themselves as authorities. Sometimes they so lack popular support that they have to seek foreign assistance. Their own internal defensive responses inevitably make them defensive against demands and values voiced in world society, such as those affecting human rights and adequate political representation. They, therefore, become defensive in their external policies also. Probably the integration end of the scale is reached only when the separate units are themselves integrated. This suggests that we should look more closely at the role of state authorities.

8. *The role of state authorities*

We have moved from the first part of our analysis which was concerned only with the malign effects of differentiation of power and false perception, to the second part in which we considered the integrative and cooperative behaviour of states. Now we assess the contemporary and future role of state authorities in world society. But we are still working on the basis of the traditional belief that world society is essentially a system of states. We will later move to a third part of our analysis which will lead us to consider how significant is state behaviour, and whether our image of world society comprising states is an accurate one. In the meantime, it is important to bear in mind the possibility that state behaviour alone neither offers adequate explanations or solutions of the problems of world society.

In terms of our analysis so far, the role of state authorities, or for that matter tribal rulers, is both defensive and integrative with respect to the wider environment in which the political unit exists. We are familiar with behaviour in the defensive role. History books are full of it: defence against adverse foreign influences, protection against foreign competition, and preservation of national cultures and institutions are the kinds of behaviour with which state authorities have historically been associated. Even internally the role of state authorities has been in the past to protect society against change, for example, to provide assistance to industries threatened by altered market conditions and new technologies, to preserve existing social and political institutions and traditions, and to protect the role of interest groups – cultural, religious or industrial – that have become a part of the existing structure of society. Externally state authorities have sought to isolate their peoples from changes and influences considered by them not to be compatible with their interests.

The role of state authorities in respect to integration and cooperation is a recently developed one. In the inter-war period the typical developed state became intensely active in protecting internal industrial systems from external competition. This was restrictive intervention designed to hold workers and capital where they were at a time of high unemployment. The state apparatus, evolved largely for this purpose, was later able to respond to increasing demands for social services, some of which arose out of the oppressive conditions of the inter-war and post-war period. Gradually, and especially after 1945, the role of the state became more constructive; rehabilitation and retraining schemes, rehousing, re-equipment of industry, and education generally were post-war functions demanded of states. This set states upon a course which led them to respond to community demands, rather than to group interests: goals of welfare led to policies quite different from those traditionally promoted to protect group interests. Consumer interests began to offset group interests in demands for protection. The modern welfare state is more and more acting as a buffer against change, and less and less as a barrier to it. The welfare state is not, as popularly conceived, one in which benefits are given wholly within the context of social services, but one in which authorities intervene to assist those affected by change to adjust to it, thus spreading the burden of change suffered by some across the whole society. The intention is not to prevent change; on the contrary, it is necessary at times to promote it as part of the adjustment process.

The defensive role of states is fully developed. No policy area has been given more attention than defence against undesired external influences – economic, cultural or military. Strategic studies is a discipline of its own. Defence strategists have received a lot of publicity. Lawyers, historians, journalists and strategists have until recently dominated the study of international relations, and from a national or state point of view. Unfortunately, the defensive role has been studied and developed almost in isolation from the integrative role of states, so much so that politically it is sometimes dangerous for political leaders to promote trade and cultural relations with other states against which the defence systems are directed. Yet private enterprise, scientists, tourists, migrants, artists and governments on a large scale have had the role of promoting actively functional cooperation between states. A study of world society is incomplete without due attention to the techniques of integration, where they succeed and where they fail.

In order to do this we must examine the notions of 'national interest' and 'rationality'; we need to appreciate the significance of role behaviour and to understand the difference between a legal and a legitimized status. Then we can turn to more detailed aspects of state decision-making.

(i) National interest

'National interests' and the interests of pressure groups within the state have formed an important part of the traditional literature concerned with International Relations. 'National interests' are those which are reflected in policies: they are the priorities as determined by authorities. Policies are justified by reference to 'the national interest'. The older laissez-faire idea was that the national interest reflected the sum total of all interest groups and was the outcome of freedom of action. Just as the free working of the competitive system was supposed to promote the greatest welfare, so the free working of the political system was supposed to result in an expression of national interests. However, apart from security and survival, there have been few wholly accepted 'national interests'. The concept of 'national interest' is not a useful one. It is a carry-over from a period in which states were relatively isolated, and their international relations were limited to acquisition of territories, defence of positions and security. It was then reasonable to discuss whether, for example, imperialism was in the national interest.[32] Now 'national interest' includes all kinds of aims and ambitions by all kinds of people, some identifying strictly with national symbols and values, and others more concerned with the progress of science, with human development, and with breaking down state barriers.

In addition to this difficulty in determining what is believed to be 'the national interest' at any given time, it is never clear whether what is thought to be the national interest is so in practice. Defence systems are created in the national interest, or an alliance is entered into. But if, as a consequence, other states react and an arms race occurs, then the result could be destructive to national interests. The consequences of policies are rarely forecast accurately – frequently they are self-defeating. Almost all decisions have unexpected consequences. We support the local supermarket: it is convenient, quick, goods are well displayed and there is a wide selection. One consequence, which we may not have anticipated, is that when an unexpected guest arrives at an hour at which the supermarket is not open and we need something, the small corner shop is no longer there. We cannot have it replaced. We have taken one decision with all kinds of consequences, changing the commercial and social structure in ways desirable and undesirable. In the same way action claimed to be in the 'national interest' can always be challenged. The only practical definition of national interest is that which authorities at the time believe to be the national interest.

Later we will give consideration to values, especially values that might be universal. We will then arrive at a more useful concept of national interests by considering them in the wider context of values. National interests will take on a different meaning – those responses to the world environment which avoid self-defeating consequences by being in conformity with trends and values that finally control behaviour universally.

When we turn to interest groups within the state, and within world society, we are on firmer ground. These are specific. We can examine how they bring pressure to bear on authorities, and we can make comparative studies of pressure groups in different states. There is an extensive literature on interest groups of all kinds.[33] There are also studies that show that they exist in free and controlled political systems, though taking different forms.

A description of interest groups does not tell us how influential they are, and to what extent they are responsible either for the structure of world society or for events that occur within it. We are accustomed to hearing dramatic assertions that certain businesses, religions or races are the cause of all our troubles, and how some determine the policies of governments behind the scenes. However, interest groups tend to offset each other – the activities of one stimulate oppositions, as when industrial interests and the pressures of organizations opposed to defence expenditure clash. Decision-making is a complex process, as will be realized when we discuss role behaviour and decision-making. Interest groups are merely one element.

Consideration of interests is, however, of particular relevance to a discussion of integrative processes. Interest groups are not always, and perhaps not primarily, national. Pressures on authorities to preserve policies of cooperation and integration are supported by trading, financial, religious, scientific, cultural and other interests. Formal decisions on matters of international interest are taken by state authorities, and their role therefore appears to be significant. It is state authorities that are finally responsible for decisions at UNESCO, World Health, GATT and at other functional institutions; they are responding to interest groups that extend beyond state boundaries. State authorities become the means of formal expression of needs and objectives pursued in the wider world society: they appear as if they were determining national policy, whereas they are more usually responding to expressions of interest that are common within the national and the world society. The social exchange model is inadequate as a model of this kind of behaviour, and even the modifications made by consideration of comparative costs and inter-dependence do not provide an adequate image of state behaviour in world society. We can see how consideration of national interest points to the integrative role of state authorities, and away from a defensive and protective role.

(ii) Rationality

Another conventional view has been that governments, and more particularly some leaders, sometimes act irrationally, or not in their or the nation's interests. By this is usually meant, not that the persons concerned are unbalanced, but that they have acted in ways that did not achieve their declared objectives. Wars have been started and lost. It has been thought that the reason may be found in the influences of pressure groups, an unfortunate selection of advisers of strong prejudices. Journalistic accounts of leaders and their personal idi-osyncracies promote this view.

A most sophisticated view is that decision-makers think and act rationally as individuals, but sometimes act irrationally as a group, a cabinet or a government. This is one way of explaining 'irrational' behaviour by otherwise obviously rational and intelligent people. One scholar has referred to the decision by Japanese leaders to join in the war on the side of Germany against the Western allies and the Soviet Union. It was argued that there is evidence that the leaders as individuals were against this decision which they, nevertheless, took as a group.

However, this is a misunderstanding of the decision-making pro-cess. We will later discuss 'role behaviour'. As individuals these Japanese leaders might have thought that an attack on Pearl Harbour and invasion of South East Asia was immoral, unlawful, too risky, too costly, and generally not to their liking. The 'pressures' on them would be personal friendships in America and Britain, codes of behaviour, religious norms, military knowledge and so on. But as a group, a cabinet or a government they were enacting a different role. They were taking responsibility for the nation, they were reacting to pressures from commercial firms who could not export manufactured textiles and other products because Western countries had excluded Japan from Asian colonial markets as a means of protecting their exports during the Great Depression. They were reacting to pressures of population. They were responding to a sense of injustice widespread in this poor community. A previous government had failed to break through the restrictions imposed on Japanese trade. Diplomatic and commercial negotiations had failed. These decision-makers, regardless of their personal views, had no option but to threaten and then adopt military means.

Their behaviour was not irrational. The war was ultimately lost, it is true. In point of fact, Japan subsequently achieved its war aims. It now trades freely throughout South East Asia, and the political structure of the countries of South East Asia has been changed in Japanese favour by reason of their occupation and the removal of colonial and feudal administrations. The revolution which their occupation commenced continues still. Clearly the Japanese decision-makers of the day could not foresee this result. But the pressures – let us call them system pressures and later define that term – led them to act as they did. They seemed to have no option, and the long-term result was in Japanese favour, even though at great cost in Japanese lives.

Apart from the fact that in the long term Japanese action did not prove irrational, the concept is inappropriate. There is no rationality or irrationality about a great deal of decision-making. One minor decision leads to another, and each is taken as the result of complex processes and a variety of influences. There is a response by the total political system to its environment. In each case of individual decision the response is the most relevant one in the prevailing circumstances – that is, in the light of the knowledge available about the environment, perceptions of the environment, values being pursued, estimates of costs of attaining these objectives, and such factors. There may be different levels of efficiency in decision-making, but this is not the same as saying that decision-making is 'irrational'. The analogy with neurotic or unreasonable individuals is not one which helps in an understanding of state behaviour in world society.

'Irrationality' also has some normative implications. We tend to think of behaviour being irrational when we disagree with it, when it does not conform with our cultural norms and codes of behaviour. Japanese behaviour was seen to be aggressive and unlawful in addition to being unsuccessful militarily. Similar military behaviour designed to protect existing structures, action in self-defence, is held in the Charter of the United Nations as lawful – at least until the Security Council can assume responsibility.[34] United States' behaviour in Vietnam was regarded as rational, and the National

Liberation Front action as irrational, by many Western observers. This was a cultural and political view. Even though they were to lose the war, the behaviour of the NLF must have been regarded by them as rational as they were fighting for freedom from a form of government they wished to reject, and from foreign influence. The term 'irrational' therefore is one which should be avoided in relation to the behaviour of large groups, communities and nations.

There is a second interest in 'irrational' behaviour, and this is a methodological one. Some scholars have argued that it is impossible to have a science of behaviour at the world society level because political behaviour is not always rational. What is really meant is that behaviour is not predictable. If we knew enough about values, role behaviour and decision-making we would probably be able to predict behaviour reliably, and then it would appear to be 'rational'. This is really at the heart of arguments about 'determinism'. Political philosophers have argued that behaviour is explicable once we know enough about it. This does not mean, necessarily, that individual freedom of choice does not occur.

Let us go back to our social exchange model, and the modifications we introduced to take account of gains from exchange. Clearly there is always a dilemma. Exchange has negative and positive advantages in relation to independence. Authorities must make a value judgement – whether the gains outweigh the loss of independence. When once the Indian Government rejected wheat from the United States which was to be given on certain conditions, it took the decision that the gains from the gift were less than loss of independence of political action. Americans might have regarded this as 'irrational'. Biafra's continued opposition to Nigeria, despite terrible losses, appeared 'irrational'. In the conduct of inter-state politics it must be assumed that behaviour is rational, and if it appears to be irrational this is because the observer is not aware of some value judgements or the perception of the actor of his environment. When a government perceives 'irrational' behaviour, this should be a warning – a warning that there are factors of which it is not aware. If policy decisions are taken in these circumstances they are likely to be unsuccessful or self defeating. The United States misjudged China before the revolution, and it has continued to misjudge it since. It misjudged the motivations and determination of the North Koreans and the North Vietnamese. It has perceived events from its own viewpoint – and many Chinese, Vietnamese and other policies have appeared to be 'irrational'. Equally, China, North Korea and North Vietnam find it difficult to interpret American policies as rational except within the purely ideological framework of imperialism. Our behaviour is always 'rational'. It is only the behaviour of others that is 'irrational'.

There is a pattern of behaviour that is clearly not in the 'national interest' and which is nevertheless 'rational'. This occurs when authorities act to preserve their own personal and group interests, to preserve themselves in office, or otherwise deliberately act against the 'national interest', even as they see it, to secure some special goal. For convenience this has been termed 'non-rational' behaviour.

(iii) Roles

Mention has already been made of role behaviour. We all enact many different roles – as a member of a school class, a church, a club, society and others. Sometimes rules that govern our behaviour in one role are not observed in another. Some people would not think of dodging train fares, but the same people might try to dodge income tax. The public revenue suffers in both cases. The leader of a political party declares his policy before an election, but once successful he pursues different policies in his role as head of government.

Journalists and some historians tend to interpret policies and motivations by reference to the known history and attitudes of persons. This can be misleading. Formal decision-makers, such as presidents and prime ministers, are subjected to a great variety of pressures and advices. They must respond to these influences if they are to continue to fulfil the requirements of their office. They may find it necessary to act in ways which seem to be out of character.

The extent to which persons can alter the role in which they act, and the extent to which personalities are affected by the role, is always difficult to determine. Was Stalin's character responsible for 'Stalinism', or was the position of the Soviet Union such that 'Stalinism' was required so as to promote industrialisation and security? Perhaps in many cases the political processes and pressures are such that persons most relevant to the required role come to the top; Hitler may have been required in conditions of mass unemployment and industrial chaos. Perhaps, also, some persons outlive their usefulness in a particular role when role requirements change. Many African leaders seem to have led their people to independence with overwhelming support, and then in independence to have acted in ways which were repressive and irrelevant. Political processes fall behind political needs, whether they be election or revolutionary processes, and there are usually significant periods in which personalities and role requirements are incompatible. Political unrest occurs, and attempts by the occupiers of the positions of authority to defend their positions can lead to repression and finally to revolt.

There are many aspects of role behaviour worth thinking about. Some of the important causes of prejudice and poor personal and group relations stem from a failure to appreciate the significance of 'role'. At a personal level – and the similarities with behaviour at the international level are obvious – we tend to have an absolutist attitude to people. They must please us in all respects, or put negatively, some behaviour which we dislike puts us off people in all their behaviour. A man in his role of football player might be objectionable; but if we knew him only in his role as debater or mechanic he might be most acceptable. Sometimes we cannot make up our minds about people just because we do differentiate their role behaviour – sometimes we like them, sometimes not. But why should we make up our minds about a person as a whole personality – unless we want to marry him or her, or enter into some partnership relationship which spreads over many roles? Our relationships are almost always with persons in particular roles, and it is their behaviour in that role that is relevant. There is a possibility that behaviour we do not like is behaviour we do not understand, or to which we are not accustomed. It is a wise safeguard not to allow some role behaviour to determine our attitude to other role behaviour. Class and race prejudice stem very largely from generalization from one role: we do not like some strange eating or religious habits so we do not like that person and his race. We do not like some strange national music and dancing – perhaps because we do not understand it – so we do not like the nationals themselves. This is absurd, but it is nevertheless true. It is almost as bad as saying, 'Billy played Caliban in Shakespeare's *Tempest,* and he appeared to be a terrible person in that role, therefore we do not like Billy off the stage.' Each person is many people. Some we like, some we may not like.

This relates to a very important theory of integration and cooperation called 'functionalism'. The argument is that people can work together most easily on functional, occupational and technical matters, and by working together in these roles, they begin to know and understand each other in other roles. If you were on the stage with Billy and saw how well he changed his personality when acting, your admiration of him and respect for him would lead you to cooperate with him. In any event, on stage you would have a common task. Off stage some of your admiration and some of the habit of working together would persist, and you would cooperate despite some personal characteristics you did not like.

In world society 'functionalism' has grown in importance since the last war. The United Nations agencies cover almost all activities, health, agriculture, civil aviation, telecommunications, labour and cultural relations, to name but a few. State authorities that are hostile to each other have representatives on these that cooperate closely on a technical basis. 'Functionalists' believe that this form of cooperation will spread until almost all relationships are dealt with at this level of technical experts who respect each other in this role.[35]

Consequently, whether we are analysing persons, groups, races, religious sects, nations or states, it is more realistic, and it is also important in practice, to be aware always of 'role behaviour'. Governments and political leaders are enacting many different roles almost simultaneously, and we will understand their behaviour and be able to predict behaviour only by determining roles.

(iv) Legitimization
At this point it is necessary to draw a distinction between legal and legitimized authorities. We have been so brought up with the idea that the authorities in government are the 'legal' authorities, that we have not paid much attention to the source of their authority. A dictator who has obtained political power by eliminating all opposition can be the legal authority, especially if other authorities recognize him as such. But has he a legitimized status, apart from this recognition by others – has he a legitimized status accorded him by those over whom he exercises authority? May it not be right and proper to defy his laws? If this is the case with a dictator, may it not be the case in respect of *some* laws decreed by a popularly elected authority? Where does one draw the line? This is clearly an important question in domestic politics; but we have not thought about it much in connection with state behaviour in world society. In what circumstances is it appropriate for one state authority to give assistance to another state authority which finds itself experiencing revolt? Is it sufficient for the state authority to be the legal one – or should there be some other test? When there is civil war, should assistance be given automatically by one legal authority to another, and not to the rebels? The British Government seemed to argue that it had some obligation to assist the 'legal' Nigerian authorities against the 'rebel' Biafrans.

Let us examine these issues. To do so we must look more closely at the nature of authority. A great amount had been written on this subject during the last century, and it is once again receiving attention, especially since 'authority' is being challenged in society generally, and on university campuses in particular. Furthermore, there is good reason to believe that a great deal, if not most international conflict, is a spill-over of domestic challenges to authority. The notions of legal, legitimate and authority are so important that we need to examine them in more depth than we have been able to examine others.

The German sociologist, Max Weber (1864–1920), studied law and then economics. He was particularly interested in the problem of freedom and authority. He believed that authority was of three kinds. There was a 'rational-legal authority' exercised over people generally, leaders and their administrations, by the legal order and structure of society itself. Individuals in their various legal and administrative roles were respected and their authority acknowledged. Another form of authority was 'traditional authority'. Practices and institutions had always existed, and authority was derived from the traditions established. Authority was not imposed by some legal authority: it was exercised by persons to whom loyalty was due, provided they reflected the known traditions. The third source of authority was 'charismatic authority' – an authority that had its source in the personality and status accorded to a leader. Such authority could be exercised against an established legal order or tradition. This form of authority clearly could not have permanency, and even during the rule of the charismatic leader usually had to be supported by reliance on religion and force. It was a type of authority associated with changing conditions and once change was accomplished, was not relevant to a new stability. There could be no loyalty of an administration to a continuing system – loyalty had to be to the person.

These are analytical types. Authority in practice includes elements of each. Weber thought that there was always a tendency for rational-legal authority to give place to traditional authority, and in conditions of change, sometimes to charismatic authority. Discipline, or the exercise of authority, tends to provoke resistances and resentments, especially if it does not accommodate to changing circumstances. The more 'stable' a society the more difficult it is to accommodate to change.

Weber was in essence adopting a traditional view of political life, while being aware of its complications. He had a belief in the 'rightness of the law'. He had a clear concept of a 'legal order': a bureaucracy, compulsory jurisdiction in the settlement of disputes and monopoly of the legitimate use of force. In more detail:

1 an administrative and legal order subject to change by legislation;
2 an administrative apparatus to conduct business in accordance with legislative regulations;
3 binding authority over all persons; and
4 the use of force within limits set by the legally constituted government.

Some scholars think that Weber diagnosed the problem of authority but finally outlined a legal order which begged some of the main questions. Talcott Parsons, commenting on Weber in 1937, paid attention to power which he described as the 'generalised capacity to secure the performance of binding obligations...'[36] In his view obedience to a leader is conditioned upon his undertaking, tacitly, to reciprocate later on with benefits. In his view legitimacy of authority came from expectations people had of future benefits. There had to be a consensus of approach. The more coercion was required to achieve compliance, the greater would be the numbers of people required to coerce. He seemed to be pointing to degrees of legitimization – authority could be partly legitimized.

Neither Weber nor Parsons seemed to be tackling the problem of minority opinion. As we know, today's minority can be tomorrow's majority. Minority opinion is often a valuable stimulus to social development. Furthermore, they seemed to equate opposition with minority opinion. There can be majority opposition opinion. Whether it is minority or majority, it is opposition. How to accommodate it is what is bothering world society today. Vietnam, Nigeria, Rhodesia, South Africa, Cyprus – all matters of international concern, and all based on minority or majority opposition to 'legal' authority.

Scholars have more recently been trying to understand problems of authority and change by looking in more detail at social processes. One scholar believes that the real test of legitimacy is the degree to which authority can handle change, and manage to achieve a new social structure.[37] He sees society as evolving in the sense that additional groups are entering into political decision-making – women, peasants, industrial workers and others who are gradually gaining more influence. Crises of legitimacy occur and authorities must be effective in handling them: an authority can lack legitimacy yet be effective.

Other scholars believe that legitimacy is not derived from threat or force but from values held by individuals: legitimacy is not something that can be attributed to authorities or a political structure as a whole.

Some aspects may be legitimized and some not. This is getting nearer to our conception of roles: in some roles authority is acceptable, and in others not so.[38] Yet other writers describe legitimacy of authority in terms of social exchange: if there is a true reciprocity, if authority provides a service of value, then there will be a legitimized status.[39] Others relate legitimization to justice.[40]

So, all in all, a variety of questions are being asked as a test of legitimacy. Was the government elected by due processes? Is authority being exercised within the limits set by the constitution or by convention? Is there a consensual or majority approval? Is authority effective? Are new entrants into the political process being accommodated? What are the areas of discontent? Does the structure of society and acquisition of political power through an absence of reciprocity cause dissent? Is there justice? Perhaps the only final measure of a serious absence of legitimization is the number of people in jail for political offences, the use of preventive detention, the repression of minority viewpoints and acts of this kind.

Let us return to the problem of intervention mentioned earlier. Clearly it is not enough for authorities in one state to give support to authorities in another merely because the latter is the legal or recognized government. The legitimized status of authorities requiring assistance is the important consideration. It is important to world society generally, because intervention to protect authorities lacking a legitimized status runs counter to observation of human rights and to the processes of adjustment to change. It is also important to the state giving the assistance. Terrible mistakes can be made, at great cost in lives, if only the 'legal' criteria are considered – as the United States has found in Vietnam. It is far from clear what form of government in that country would have a legitimized status: authorities of this type emerge only gradually. But it is clear that the legal government to whose aid the United States originally came, lacked such a status.

Later we shall be discussing values, arguing that some values are probably held universally. We may become clearer about the notion of legitimization then.

(v) Decision-making

Decision-making has received the special attention of scholars during the last two decades. Models of decision-making, showing input, perception, the processes of storage of information, information retrieval, output, response to the environment, new inputs, and so on, have been found to have a general application in business management, domestic politics and international relations. Decision-making in crises, comparative studies between planned and free economies, decision-making latitude and others have been studied in detail.

There is no particular aspect of traditional international relations studies that better shows how thought has developed than decision-making. In 1954 a young scholar, unhappy with the form of exposition used to describe the 'power theories' of the period immediately following the Second World War, put forward a simple input-output model.[41] He endeavoured to translate power theories into a more precise analysis of the resources at the disposal of authorities, and the ways in which they employed these to achieve their goals. This model did not include an analysis of the process by which authorities come to their decisions.

In the meantime other scholars were examining 'decision-making as an approach to the study of international affairs'. A paper by this title was published in 1954, and subsequently developed in a book on foreign policy decision-making in 1962.[42] The belief was that by examining the process of making decisions much could be learned about world society. The simple Modelski model of inputs and outputs gave place to complex diagrams showing environmental influences on decision-making. Since then there have been further developments. In 1963 another scholar made a major contribution by emphasising the way in which responses by the environment (other states) fed back into decision-making, just as the presence of clouds and storms feeds back into the electronic navigator systems of aircraft.[43] This process was found to be common to all systems, and was spelled out in 1965 by another scholar who endeavoured to apply a systems analysis to political relations.[44] More recently it has been realised that two systems, apparently the same, can respond to the same event differently. Though they appear to be much the same, as is the case with many individuals and state authorities, they are 'programmed' by their experiences and culture to perceive or interpret what they perceive quite differently.[45] Once the study of world society reached this point, it was a short step to a consideration of 'values', that is, the motivations and goals that help to control what is perceived. We will be spelling out this development in thinking in more detail when we consider values.

There has been a specialized interest in decision-making in times of crisis. By a crisis is meant (a) a situation that is largely unforeseen, at least unforeseen in all its details though perhaps not wholly unexpected, (b) one in which there is a critical time by which a decision is required, and (c) one in which the decision involves options that risk damage to others. Scholars have endeavoured to trace decision-making in such times of tension, the way in which usual processes of consultation and advice are ignored, the way in which relevant information is not taken into account in the heat of the moment. Some 'crisis' situations, like the Cuban one, had the crisis features, but in practice led to careful and thoughtful analysis. The 'crisis' did not mean that facts were ignored. It probably led to a neglect of other matters that required decisions and which became crisis for want of them – perhaps racial confrontations. But interesting observations arise out of these special studies. It could be argued, for example, that if inherent in a crisis is a time factor, then authorities should avoid imposing a time on others. 'If you do not eat your lunch by noon you will be punished' creates a crisis at noon, perhaps unnecessarily.

(vi) Decision-making and the state system
It is necessary to place decision-making at the state authority level in a perspective of the wider problems of management in world society. There has been a tendency to record inter-state relations by recording decisions and actions of state authorities, and this has carried an implication that events were as they were because of these decisions, and, in particular, because of the personalities and circumstances of the day. This is, however, a journalistic approach: it is a record of events. As such it is interesting and useful for some purposes. It can be misleading as to the nature of world society, and the processes that operate within it.

Decisions taken by authorities are formal decisions. As such they have some contractual and policy implications. But they do not tell us about the decision-making processes, especially in cases in which decisions at one point of time are the consequences of decisions taken years before. President Nixon was required to take decisions regarding Vietnam immediately on assuming office, as was President Johnson before him. But each took decisions required as a result of decisions taken by others many years previously. These previous ones limit the decision-making latitude at any subsequent time. The history of Vietnam, from the point of view of United States involvement, commences with the failure of American policy which sought to support Chiang Kai-shek against the communist rebellion, and decisions taken then that communism threatened the whole of Asia. More specific decisions to give the government of South Vietnam technical assistance and advice led to a series of decisions which involved the United States more and more. Public opinion in America, once the issues and the costs had become clearer, required a de-escalation of the conflict, and once again each decision led predictably to the next. The formal decision-maker is the President, the actual decision-maker is a long and complicated process. It is this which decision-making theory attempts to analyse and describe, and on the basis of such a theory the process can be analysed and described in relation to a particular event.

Descriptions of world events that dwell on decisions taken by state authorities also carry the implication that world society is the end result of interactions among separate entities, states. Once again, state authorities are only the formal decision-makers. Decisions are, in practice, made for them by interactions at other levels. Take Vietnam again. Public opinion in the United States has been one factor. Public opinion in other states has also had its influence directly, and indirectly through governments. Scholars, students, religious organizations and institutions that operate across national boundaries have created conditions which have made certain decisions inevitable. This is world society operating, not just states, or even peoples through states. State authorities cannot in the long term isolate themselves from the influences of world society.

Even the General Assembly of the United Nations cannot be regarded as an expression of world society – it is an expression of the policies of state authorities, arrived at to some degree as a result of pressures from other states. World society can create conditions which defeat United Nations purposes, for example, sanctions against Rhodesia. World society could be regarded as the end product of decision-making by state authorities only if all state authorities were able to exercise total control of all behaviour of their citizens, and all transactions and links that cut across state boundaries. This absurd assumption is one which has been implied in traditional studies of international relations. It has given rise to an undue emphasis on the role of states, personality of decision-makers, state institutions and formal decisions at the state level. The United Nations is in some respects a closed club of state authorities seeking to preserve themselves, even, if necessary, against the interests of many peoples. For example, the United Nations seems to support one of its members against attempts by peoples within a state to form a separate government – which seemed to be the case in relation to Nigeria. We cannot assume that an international institution comprising governments reflects the interests of world society.

(vii) *The state and world society*

We have discussed the 'national interest' of states, the manner in which authorities behave in the pursuit of their interests, the way in which individuals identify with the goals they are required to seek by reason of their positions, the tendency for authorities to pursue their interests rather than to reflect the altering interests of society, and the processes by which decisions finally emerge. We are left with a most important question. Does the existence of state authorities effectively prevent cooperation in world society, or the emergence of an integrated world society, except to the extent that this may be possible within the limits imposed by state authorities? Can there be a withering away of the state in favour of an integrated world society?

Earlier we discussed the failures of collective security and other means of achieving an integrated world society based on the state system. We have also observed that there are conditions in which integration is possible, such as have made some federations practical. We discussed the influence of perception in determining the defensive or integrative posture of states. Assuming that all states perceived their relationships with others as being at the integrative end of the spectrum, what degree of integration would be possible in world society?

The assumption is itself an absurd one. To be valid it would be necessary for each state authority to be wholly responsive to the demands of its society, to be wholly legitimized, to be prepared to adapt itself to values it did not share or to remove itself. Unless this were so an authority would be fearful of external influences supporting internal oppositions, and would, therefore, be defensive and not integrative in its external behaviour. But let us make this unrealistic assumption, and see whether even in these circumstances there could be an integrated world society on the basis of a state system.

Clearly, a world society based on unified states would be a less disturbed one than the one we know. Obviously Vietnams and Nigeria-Biafra conflicts would not occur. Many other types of conflict would probably be reduced because there seems to be a tendency for authorities to react to internal political difficulties by means which create external tensions, as, for example, when restraints are imposed on the movements across boundaries of people and ideas. But ideological, cultural, racial, religious, economic and institutional differences would still exist between states even though they were unified. The traditional fears of the aggression of others would still lead to self-defeating defensive strategies. In other words, even in these conditions of political maturity of each state there would be effective limits on the degree of inter-state integration that could be attained.

Within these limits there is, of course, scope for extensive cooperation and integration on a functional basis. Even in the conditions of the real world a large number of important services are provided through international institutions. Authorities, even authorities that are in conflict on other matters, are prepared to cooperate through functional institutions such as the World Health Organization and those dealing with communications of all kinds. But even authorities in unified states would not agree to hand over to an international institution, especially one which took decisions on a two-thirds or consensual voting basis, the power to make decisions on the language that should be employed, the political institutions that should be developed, the ideologies they should promote and matters of this kind. Functional cooperation can go a long way within the state framework, but finally it comes up against the different and perhaps conflicting values of authorities and the peoples they represent. There is this important influence of local or non-universalized interests with which we must cope.

Even the most ardent advocate of world government would acknowledge that the majority of political services, such as health, education, law and order, rubbish collection and road maintenance, have to be created and administered in ways suited to local conditions. To be effective many political services need to be made available within political units far smaller than the modern nation states. Smaller and smaller political units, even going down to local council levels, are probably desirable, provided they are integrated into larger and larger economic units, and even universal units that determine common standards where this is appropriate. There are reasons for believing that the contemporary state is too big a unit to be efficient in providing political services, and in enabling effective participation in making decisions that directly affect people. 'Viable' political units are very small – as small as the tiny island of Tonga – provided they operate effectively within a wider economic system.

Perhaps the clue to our problem of altering the state basis of world society is not in universal functionalism alone, but in decentralized administration within states, combined with increasing centralization within world society of those functions, such as the control of standards and agreement on common procedures, which can serve commonly felt needs. This reduction of power at the state level, and increase in decentralized power, is a process which is possible politically. It is a reallocation of political power within a state on a functional or efficiency basis. It may be that scholars interested in world society should be paying attention to decentralization within states as the means of creating an integrated world society, and far less seeking to find means of reducing state power by superimposing international institutions. People can have many loyalties simultane-ously – loyalties to a local authority in respect of some matters, and to international institutions in respect of others.[46] Nationalism is a condition in which all loyalties are focused at the level of state authorities, and is most intense when there is threat to the state as a unit, the state being the common provider of all services, from security to education. Loyalties are attracted to sources of services, and in some developed countries today, such as the United Kingdom, there are already signs of multiple loyalties, to local government, national and state authorities and international institutions. The Common Market could attract other loyalties if it provides services.

While this may be the long term solution, we now face a security problem, if for no reason other than the political realisms of today. There are some centralized and powerful states, and very many centralized politically immature states, making integration on a decentralized and functional basis impossible. What is required of us is to determine what are the values and goals of peoples, which of these are best satisfied by local political authorities for reasons of either efficiency or cultural differences, and which are best satisfied by international institutions because of their universal nature. In the course of doing this we will probably find cases where existing institutions seem to submerge common values and allow acquired ones to dominate and divide world society.

PART THREE

Prescription

9. *Values*

We can now turn to the third part of our study. It will be recalled that we examined the ways in which differentiation of power occurred through ordinary social exchange, and how, in these conditions, mutual fears stimulated perceptions of hostility and defensive responses that were cumulative and self-defeating. Then we modified this first approach by dealing with the other side of exchange relationships, the integrative and cooperative aspects through which groups gain without necessarily loss of independence. We considered aspects of state behaviour and decision-making. It will be recalled that in embarking on this second part a warning was given – not to assume that state behaviour could provide a full explanation or understanding of world society, or, by implication, solutions to world problems. Now we turn to look at world society as a whole and modify our approach and take into account influences outside state control.

We have already seen that 'national interests' are frequently expressions of interests of nationals shared by nationals of other states, leading to common policies and functional cooperation within the inter-state system. Can we go further, are there interests held in common universally which would justify our looking at world society as a unit?

This question has two aspects. It may be true that all states have some identical interests and that there are universal interests in the inter-state system; but these interests may be incompatible nevertheless. Each state wants security and prosperity, and it may be that the security and prosperity of one means the insecurity and poverty of another. (This is not necessarily so, and later when we discuss conflict we will be referring to relations that are 'zero sum' and 'variable sum' – that is relationships in which the gain of one side is equal to the loss of the other, or in which both sides gain or lose.) Even when relations are of this nature it could be important to identify the universal or common values. Each state would at least be able to understand the behaviour of others by reference to its own. If Israel and the Arab states both appreciated that the security motivations of each other were the same, they would have more favourable impressions of the motivations of each other. We will return to consider incompatible interests.

There is a second possibility which justifies our looking at world society as a unit. It could be that people of all races and creeds have some common values and similar objectives, and furthermore, it could be that these can best be achieved by cooperation. It could be that these common values and objectives are hidden from view, and that peoples cannot cooperate in attaining them, because they are overwhelmed by the values and objectives of institutions, including states. The study of world society has concentrated on the study of institutions. We need to remind ourselves from time to time that our study is the study of man.

(i) Motivations in world society

Political theory is concerned with systems of relationships and their characteristics; the roles of actors, and the actors themselves; the decision-making processes by which scarce resources are distributed in the satisfaction of values; the state, inter-state, and private institutions that exist for the taking of and giving effect to decisions; the areas of decision-making within systems as determined by geographical boundaries and by transactions and links that cross them; constitutional and legitimized status of authorities; normative rules of behaviour; the processes by which conflicts among actors might be extended, settled, resolved, or avoided; and ways in which actors can be deterred in the pursuit of their values. These are all studies essentially of institutions and how they operate. Such studies are being pursued, sometimes in great detail, as though in them would be discovered the motivations and responses of the peoples, groups, nations, states, and other organizations that comprise societies, and the explanations of national and world society that would give us the ability to predict and to control them. But the study of politics, including world politics, is the study of perceptions that units within a society have of it and of each other, and the values, that is the objectives and preferences that are the drive to behaviour, which each holds. Perceptions are a stimulus to actions; they are responsible for expectations and for fears. Israeli and Arab perceptions of each other are a source of apprehension. To a large extent they establish the framework in which values are formulated and pursued within it. They are therefore the core topics of the study of behaviour in and of any society.

The motivations and responses of the individual Vietnamese agricultural worker after the Second World War were affected by the knowledge that feudal systems of land tenure were not the only possible ones. The fears of individual Biafrans for their lives and futures, the threats perceived by individual Arabs and Israelis, the felt resentments of individual Africans against Europeans and Asians, are the influences ultimately to be included in any explanation of international society and its altering structures. Values at these levels are specific and can be examined by social science techniques. The next step in political analysis is to ascertain which, if any, values are common in world society. Participation in decision-making, security, ethnic identity, equality of opportunity? Do social-psychological values have an absolute quality not conspicuous in institutional values: what leads men to burn themselves and to fight losing battles? Are some social-psychological values universal: is there some connection between student demands for participation and the Biafran defiance of the federal government? What are the circumstances in which participants are prepared to give support to, or alternatively to destroy, institutions in which they hold minority opinions: why do parliamentary systems survive in some circumstances and not in others? Do East and West Germans, and North and South Koreans, have different values, and if so why should peoples of the same culture have different values under different administrations? How long will these differences persist: did the different institutions create different political and social values or merely submerge some as colonialism submerged values? Did conflict in Cyprus and Nigeria occur because of fears within the communities, or because of fears promoted by ambitious leadership? There are no philosophical answers to these questions: they are empirical questions, and furthermore, they are questions that must be asked and answered at a social-psychological or a social-biological level. There is no substitute for finding out what values exist in particular situations by asking relevant people relevant questions. The relevant people are those who make up communities and help to create institutions that wholly reflect their values – legitimized institutions – and not authorities that sometimes lack legitimized status and must in due course either give place to others or alter their value systems. It would clear a great deal of philosophical argument and give us knowledge of municipal and world society if we were to get down to the job of finding whether this is so, and what the common values are.

It could be argued that extending the subject of politics to include values at all levels is to take it into the fields of psychology, anthropology, sociology and biology, and beyond any reasonable definition of the subject. This is not a tenable position. Indeed, it is the attempt to make of the study of politics and world politics something separate from other behavioural studies that has been a barrier to their development, and a source of serious misconceptions. It is not possible to explain separately different levels of behaviour – the individual, family, tribe, village, town, city, province, nation, state, and world society. Nor is it possible to make an arbitrary distinction between biology, psychology, social psychology, sociology, anthropology, politics, and international politics by reference to the numerical size of social units being examined. A behavioural analysis that took into account values at lower levels of organization, for example, values attached to participation in decision-making, would probably suggest the political and social relevance of smaller and smaller, and of more and more political units, in a world society comprising larger and larger economic ones. One has only to think of the Nigerian-Biafran struggle to realize the different policy consequences of these two different academic ways of approaching the subject of world society. From a behavioural viewpoint one would see the Biafran revolt as reflecting important values, and compatible with the basic influences in world society. There is some case for confining the study of international relations to those formal relations known to diplomatic historians, but once a political scientist moves beyond formal government-to-government transactions he is concerned with the influences that are brought to bear upon authorities, transactions other than government-to-government, and the perceptions and values of all communities small and large that directly or indirectly have a bearing upon world society. Whatever divisions of labour may be required, the separation of international politics from politics, and the separation of politics from the behavioural studies must be counterproductive.

If theories concerning the making of policy and the behaviour of systems generally take into account only institutional attributes such as system values, decision-making processes, the status of authorities, roles and other aspects of society, and neglect the motivations and responses of its members, then they are likely to have very little, if any, predictive value. The theory of the balance of power was an explanation of world society at a particular time. It depended, in theory, on states having no cultural or traditional values or links that would inhibit them from supporting one power today and another tomorrow in order to maintain a balance. For this reason alone it could not succeed. The theory of collective security, under which existing structures were to be maintained and the behaviour of smaller states controlled, took no account of changing political and social values and expectations. From time to time the system broke down, and wars occurred, under the built-up pressures of frustrated change. So today, theories and domestic policies that rest on the institutional, structural, and decision-making aspects of society but which neglect the influences that were responsible for this apparatus, must likewise fail.

(ii) Social-biological values

There has always been a wide interest in values among philosophers and political scientists. Probably no single topic has been more discussed. However, it has never been clear what precisely was being discussed. 'Values' has been used to describe the long-term aspirations of states, such as peace and prosperity; the national interests of states as perceived by authorities; immediate policy objectives; the strategies by which goals are sought; and ethnic, religious and ideological norms that are associated with different cultures and traditions. It has also been employed as a generic term to cover all the above, that is anything which is held to be valuable, the test being a willingness to expand resources in its defence or attainment. A recent usage relates to conditions necessary for the preservation of social systems; for example, the value attached to preserving rates of change that are within the capabilities of systems to absorb. General Systems Theory and the use of systems analysis have drawn attention to values of this type.[47] These are now being incorporated into political theory.[48]

These are all institutional values, that is, values that relate directly to the survival of institutions, or to the cultural goals of separately organized societies. Contemporary thinking is more concerned with social-psychological values. It is probably stimulated by political experience, such as student behaviour and struggles for independence by national groups within states, and by innovations in the handling of social problems that rest upon assessments of these values, such as social casework and the activities of probation officers.[49] These values held at individual and small-group levels include priorities and preferences such as the attainment of certain conditions of freedom, self-determination even at the expense of life itself, group integrity, equality of opportunities in education and employment, the preservation of cultures, and identity with ethnic, religious and language groups. Values at these levels are those described by creative writers who endeavour to depict the lives and drives of peoples and social groups living within their institutional frameworks. They are the preferences of people, the drives that finally underpin or destroy institutions.

In examining social-psychological values from the point of view of political science, and especially political science concerned with world society, we are not concerned only or even mainly with individually held values that are acquired and subject to change. Our interest is in those that are fundamental in human behaviour, and for this reason presumably universal. There is a distinction to be made between, on the one hand, values that people of one culture or ideology believe others should share (for example, values associated with parliamentary institutions, laissez-faire trading, and the religion of particular sects), and, on the other, values that are held by people within all cultures and ideological systems. This latter type of social-psychological values can be described as social-biological, because they are closely related to, if not direct expressions of, biological drives and motivations. They must form part of an analysis of any aspect of world society. They are a fundamental particle of human behaviour. They are connected with survival, personality development, and self-maintenance within any social environment. They are not unique to men: conformity, participation, social exchange, and such social phenomena can be observed in more primitive organisms. Social-biological values, like more basic reflex behaviour, are probably more the outcome of the information content of human organization than they are of cultural, educational, and other such influences that affect adult human behaviour. They are probably an example of 'homeostasis', that is a property that remains constant despite external forces.

Failure to distinguish between social-psychological values and social-biological ones has led us to regard social behaviour as something different in kind from physical and biological behaviour. There has been an ill-defined hypothesis that human behaviour is controlled by 'will' or some such influence that does not occur in other biological behaviour. Certainly social-psychological values change with altering conditions and different environments; cultural, religious and ideological values are evidence of this. Social-biological values have the same appearance of alteration or emergence, but this is probably due to altering environmental conditions that allow them to find expression. It may be that we have mistakenly regarded these values as evolving or altering over time instead of merely coming into evidence as social and political changes have taken place. We have had difficulty in explaining the widespread and apparently spontaneous nature of independence movements, political revolutions, and social rebellions that have been recorded in history. A hypothesis that there are social-biological values that are fundamental particles, parts of the information content of biological organization, serves to explain the apparently continuing struggle for participation and freedom to develop personality within a social environment. Aggressive and power drives cannot be regarded as having this same fundamental quality. They are less universal, and may be no more than a manifestation of frustrated values and evidence of the existence of more basic drives. At a political level, such a hypothesis serves to explain the persistent demand for independence of nations, and for identification of groups within states. These manifestations of nationalism have clear biological origins and protective functions.

There is a supposition here that, in the course of social evolution, basic drives and motivations have been suppressed by institutional restraints, initially of a purely social or community character, and later by those resulting from economic specialization and organization. In accordance with this supposition, the overt expression of values that characterize every level of contemporary municipal and world society is a reaction against this institutional overlay. This is the nature of challenge to authority with which we are familiar. In other words, there is a supposition that social-institutional development includes an interaction between the expression of values and their control, and that either one can be the dominant influence in some localities, and in some periods of time.

In relatively stable and satisfied political communities the process of political socialization effectively channels and controls social-biological drives.[50] Where, however, there are ethnic communities that feel threatened, economic groups that feel prejudiced, or minorities that have no means of effective participation in political decisions, there is reduced political socialization. This applies as much, if not more, to highly developed industrial societies as to underdeveloped ones where the problem of alienation is becoming acute.

Nor is social-biological behaviour an attribute of less educated peoples. There is a qualitative difference between reflex or instinctive behaviour – used in the common sense of basic drives – and social-biological value behaviour. Instinctive behaviour is restrained by cortical dominance or control by intellectual processes, as required by the social environment. A good deal of it is irrelevant to survival in a civilized social setting. For example, there are social responses to threat that do not necessarily require violence, as for example, calling for police help. Value behaviour, on the other hand, is more and not less relevant to survival and personality development as the social environment becomes more highly organized. It is not subject to the same cortical control. On the contrary, cortical dominance helps to stimulate, and to direct it sometimes into aggressive and even destructive activity. Hence violent student demonstrations.

One of the normative corollaries of the hypothesis that some types of values are incorporated in the information content of organisms, and have this special qualitative feature, is that suppression of social groups, and denial of political participation and of equality of opportunity, are possible only in the short term, and in particular circumstances. Institutions that prevent the expression of value behaviour are under constant threat. The legitimized status and authority of institutions is finally derived from value behaviour at this sociological-biological level.

On this reasoning, observation of situations, and the making of policy, could be subjected to rules based on homeostasis. Prediction of behaviour, in given circumstances, and over periods of time, could come within statistical probability. Indeed, intuitively we are coming to this view by reason of experience such as that in Vietnam, where expectations of behaviour based on power theories with little reference to values have been shown to be false. Eastern European history in the last decade has also stimulated thought about the nature and persistence of social-psychological and social-biological values in particular.

(iii) Schizophrenic attitudes to values

Even where it is generally accepted that the right of participation in decision-making or the right of association, is a widely held value and a human 'right', the exercise of this right by others is none the less often resisted within and between groups. Other values or institutional norms of behaviour are invoked, such as values associated with particular forms of law and order, and they are held to be overriding and to justify the suppression of these social-psychological values. The drives and motivations of people are thus suppressed by institutional and cultural values. The reason for this conflict between human values and institutional norms is not hard to find. Specialization in social exchange leads to loss of independence and to relations based on bargaining and power. Institutionalized norms then serve to legitimize and preserve the resultant social structures. Normative sanctions emerge as the means of controlling power relationships. In these circumstances the motivations and responses of others – even though they are identical with one's own – come to be regarded as a threat to existing institutions and positions of privilege. Indeed they are: there is a latent conflict between changing values and state institutional norms. The pursuit of their values by some actors is interpreted by others as ideology and even irrationality. In historical and political writings values are sometimes treated as being among influences in world society that should be curbed, and against which institutions of restraint should be directed. Nationalism, which is a universal and integrative force in social organization, has accordingly been perceived as though it were a malign influence in world society. In the course of time it is institutions and norms that must adapt to values. Consequently, the study of biological values, in particular, has a predictive potential, and for this reason needs to be incorporated in political theory.

Municipal and world society have both been regarded – and are still widely viewed – by men of affairs and by many scholars as comprising institutions within which members are required to conform to traditional patterns of behaviour. The institution of feudalism, and the institutions of capitalism and socialism, required – and still require – a high degree of conformity, and human values were – and still are – submerged and even sacrificed to institutional values. Education, communications, rising expectations of participation in decision-making, and the welfare state are among influences that have helped to bring individual and group values to the surface. Acceptance by people of existing circumstances has diminished with knowledge of what is possible. What was once thought by the individual to be a natural order is now seen to be subject to change by human protest and political organization. Independence movements, student protest, and the growing North-South confrontation, are particular symptoms of the emergence of an expression of values at levels lower than institutions. The development of social studies, especially those dealing with individual and group responses to environmental conditions, such as neuroses, delinquencies, learning, and adjustment, have helped further to focus attention on behavioural values rather than institutional ones.

It is not only closed societies that have been preoccupied by institutional values; world society has comprised state units that paid high regard to institutional values, and was structured in ways that submerged all other outlooks and objectives. Until a few decades ago world society effectively comprised a relatively small number of states each dominated by one of a few greater ones. States could then reasonably be considered as the main actors, and, as such, entities. Sovereignty, rules of war and neutrality, protection of nationals of great powers, and treaty rights and privileges of great powers were the main subjects of discussion, negotiation and study. The human interests and values of peoples in smaller states and colonies were not politically important. World politics could then reasonably be described and explained in the simple terms of the interests of powerful and hegemonial states to which smaller states and subject peoples had to accommodate themselves. In municipal and in world society, values were relevant only to the extent that they were a by-product of power.

Understandably, theories of political behaviour were based upon an acceptance of human struggles as being related to some natural and inevitable aggressiveness. Even today little attention is paid in foreign-policy making to the values of others. We are content to refer to the pursuit by others of their values as a form of aggressiveness or anti-social behaviour to be curbed by national and international restraints. It is only in academic political analysis, and not always there, that it is acknowledged that individual and group behaviour of a type that does not conform with normative patterns is sometimes explicable in terms of values that are as strongly held, and as important to those holding them, as the values which our own society has traditionally accepted. The emergence of new nations, and the surfacing of cultures and behavioural patterns previously submerged by European and indigenous overlords, are causing scholars to entertain the idea that the responses that politically have been regarded as 'aggressive', for example, nationalist movements, revolts against feudal systems, and resistance to racial discrimination, may be to those concerned their inevitable responses to the perceived environmental conditions in the light of the knowledge available. Perhaps they are sometimes the only politically practicable responses to a set of intolerable options that have been imposed by the environment – that is, by other groups, nations, and states. We are just beginning, intellectually, to understand the significance of values in a world structure which contains no in-built processes of gradual change for the satisfaction of values, except those that involve violence. There has been an important shift in the study of world society in the last few decades from a normative approach to one that analyses and endeavours to understand political response, violent or non-violent, as a reaction to an environment, a major part of which is the behaviour of other actors. The values of the units being observed are beginning to be the object of analysis, even though as yet they are still grossly described, and usually at an institutional level. It is this which has made political science both more realistic and more exciting as a study, and far more complex. The study of politics is no longer history or the study of organization; it is the study of behaviour in all its human aspects.

(iv) Values and the history of thought

On this reasoning it is possible to interpret more satisfactorily the history of thought in politics and international politics. Waltz postulated three images: man, the state, and the international system.[51] In each of these are origins of conflict, and each diagnosis suggests a remedy. Man has been assumed to be aggressive, and the remedy is his conversion to a set of norms, or his control. The state was thought to be an origin of conflict, by some because it intervened and endeavoured to control, by others because it did not control enough. The inter-state system was merely an extension of the institutions of state defence, through which powerful states could control the behaviour of other peoples. Other images have emerged since Waltz wrote in the 1950s. One is the decision-making image, which recognizes the need to take into account the response of the environment, and other cybernetic processes of decision-making. It is an image that departs from the three previous ones in that decision-making is no longer seen as a simple power input and distribution: decision-making within a power framework can be more successful if account is taken of feedback from the environment. The values of others, even though they are values at an institutional level, are seen to be relevant. Associated with this image is a change in the model employed, from the billiard-ball model of the previous images, to a systems one based on cross-national transactions. Another recent image is the social change and spill-over image, which attributes conflict to struggles within states that spill over into international conflict. This directs attention to the conflict within political structures between institutional and social-psychological values. What is suggested here is a sixth image, one that substitutes fundamental and perhaps universal values as explanations of behaviour at the individual and state levels, and thus even further breaks down any distinction between political behaviour within and among states.

Perceived reality in world society

Sources of conflict	Axioms and hypotheses	Remedies	Mediation
1 Man	Aggressiveness: original sin: acquisitiveness	Conversion to normative rules: coercion: education: partitions	Judicial settlements and enforcement
2 State	Laissez-faire and the common good: control of groups in interests of whole: aggressiveness as racial characteristic: self-fulfilling prophecies and self-defeating strategies	Defences: alliances	Compromise
3 Inter-state systems	Fixed sum relations: power as determinant of relations: billiard-ball model: legality: conflict as accident: conflict in ideology and personality	Power balances: collective security: world government: deterrence	Good offices and mediation: peace-keeping: traditional international law and enforcement: great power influence
4 Decision-making	Failures of decision-making: communication and cybernetic processes: role theory	Conflict avoidance by improved theory and training: increased information	Exploration of alternative goals and means
5 State politics	Continuing domestic political and social unrest: spill-over: world society as systems: boundaries: ethnic communities: race and class	Internal social and political change: non-intervention: neutralization and nonalignment: world consensus and domestic jurisdiction	Peace-keeping during planned change
6 Values	Variable sum relations: perception: institutional and human values: social-psychological values: mass media and political socialization: legitimization	Reperception: reassessment of values and costs: functional cooperation: prediction as a means of conflict avoidance	Supportive techniques: control of communication: official, hidden and unconscious objectives: two audience problem: avoidance of compromise: conflict or a problem to solve

(v) The practical importance of values

There are some practical reasons for stressing a value approach to politics, in addition to methodological ones. Social-psychological values are essentially subjective phenomena: it is their existence that gives to politics whatever flexibility or non-deterministic features it has. They are subjective in the sense that they are arrived at within a framework of perceived opportunities, whether or not the opportunities in some realistic sense occur. They are also subjective in the sense that these values are themselves given relative values, thus forming a value system or set of priorities. Because they are subjective they are also subject to change and manipulation. By working on values, institutions and relationships can be altered; but values cannot as readily be changed by working on institutions and relationships. An institutional approach to society leads to structures designed to ensure conformity with some preconceived norms of behaviour, and threat, coercion and deterrence are the instruments. They can do no more than suppress or frustrate value systems. A value approach opens up quite different ways of handling conflict and relationships generally. The objective comes to be not restraint and deterrence, but ways by which actors can be helped to reassess relative values in the light of increased knowledge of the environment, of the values of others, and of the costs of pursuing immediate ones in terms of loss of other values that are likely to be incurred. A value approach takes us away from judicial and coercive settlements to the type of adjustments that are made out of court by social caseworkers, psychiatrists, industrial mediators and others who have found that adjustment to an environment and the avoidance of conflict are most directly and permanently effected by adjustments within the actors themselves. The extension of a value approach to international conflict along the lines of the contemporary approach to small-group conflict is one that is only now being explored.[52] Social-biological values are universal and provide a basis on which parties in conflict can identify with each other and begin to understand the notion of mirror images. Parties in conflict struggle to attain the same values – security and certainty. But these are not scarce products. Their availability is increased by functional cooperation in securing them.

There are important academic implications in this. No behavioural study can advance beyond an early theorizing stage in the absence of clinical conditions in which there can be recorded observations and testing of hypotheses based on them. Even if a political scientist could work within a number of foreign offices, he could not gain much information about the nature of world society, though he would have some knowledge about some aspects of the total process of decision-making. Nor could he gain much from seeing the inside of international institutions. Neither would give insights into motivations and responses. However, if he sets out to examine values at all levels there are opportunities for field studies and direct involvement. He can undertake field studies in communal relationships that spill over into international ones, in relations between authorities and minorities that no less have a spill-over effect in an environment of power rivalries such as the present, and in racial and other such conflicts. He can employ attitude studies that are designed to ascertain the main fears and aspirations that lie behind responses to the environment. At both social and official levels he can gain knowledge of motivations and response by bringing together representatives of opposing viewpoints, both within communities and between states, to see to what extent the perceptions and values of each party can be altered by increased information about the perceptions and values of the opposing party. This is a clinical research framework.

We now need to look ahead to the next century. World society will alter more and more with increases in communications, travel, knowledge and scientific discovery. The problems of the future are population increases leading to growing inequalities of real income, desperate defence of privilege by Western peoples, conflicts over social and political change and challenge to authorities at state and world levels. The study of decision-making processes at state levels cannot help us in analysing and predicting this kind of development.

10. *Conflict*

'The substance of international politics is conflict and its adjustment among groups of people who acknowledge no common supreme authority.'[53] Conflict has featured in historical records, and is the popular reason for an interest in world affairs. One of the conscious purposes of the study of world society is to analyse, to understand and hopefully to find means of resolving conflict.

Having examined world society as a system of states, and also in the broader perspective of values that are universal, we can now see whether our analysis helps in an understanding of conflict. It will be a good test of our analysis.

The view that conflict is inherent in world society has been widely accepted. Some historians take the view that, like road accidents, political clashes are bound to occur. In addition to the nature of man and the competitive structure of states, there are personal and local factors that make conflicts inevitable and unpredictable. The self-defeating nature of traditional state politics, which we have examined, has seemed to confirm these views.

These are views that were widespread before there had been much analysis of world affairs, apart from that which is a by-product of description. Consideration of perceptions, role behaviour, legitimization and decision-making at the inter-state level, and of values and transactions in world society that cut across state boundaries, have begun to open up new lines of enquiry. Now many serious scholars are drawing on studies in other disciplines, carrying out empirical work, and developing peace studies – that is, studies of how to create self-supporting conditions of peace, and not merely the absence of war which is thought to be possible if there were adequate deterrents.

(i) The nature of conflict

Let us first look at conflict as a social phenomenon. Conflict, like sex, is an essential creative element in human relationships. It is the means to change, the means by which our social values of welfare, security, justice and opportunities for personal development can be achieved. If suppressed, as is often the case in traditional societies where conflict is settled according to traditionally accepted norms, society becomes static. In highly industrialized communities, rates of technological change are rapid and accelerating, and consequently conflict is widespread and fundamental. There is conflict between the individual and society, between privileged and underprivileged, between managers and managed, and between those possessing different ideological values. These conflicts challenge authorities, institutions and traditionally held values. But they are neither to be deprecated nor feared. The existence of a flow of conflict is the only guarantee that the aspirations of society will be attained. Indeed, conflict, like sex, is to be enjoyed. If such a fundamental and pervasive element in human relations were not enjoyable, there could be no human enjoyment.

We are concerned, clearly, with the management of conflict, not its elimination. We seek to retain conflict which has functional value, and to control it so as to avoid perversions which are destructive of human enjoyment and widely held social interests.

Two propositions emerge. If the functional value of conflict is to be exploited, then situations of conflict must not be prevented or settled by authorities seeking merely to conserve. Conflicts must not be suppressed by threat, and they must not be settled by reference to past norms and practices that are no longer perceived as relevant or just. The appeal to 'law and order', as though this were a goal in itself, is a dangerous one. Conflict must be resolved to the satisfaction of the parties, and for all practical purposes, by the parties. This is the first proposition.

There is, however, a social interest in the resolution of conflict. A and B do not necessarily resolve their conflict in ways compatible with the interests of the wider community. There is a legitimate interest of representative authorities in the outcome of conflict between two parties. This applies to the international as well as to the national community. In the latter case this is especially so in the industrial field. This is proposition two.

These two propositions seem to present a dilemma. On the one hand there is a need to be permissive of conflict and to resolve it in ways acceptable to the parties, and on the other there is a need to promote wider social needs. This dilemma poses two questions. The first is, how can conflict be resolved without third-party coercion,

without reliance upon conserving laws and norms, and to the satisfaction of the parties? The second question is, how can social needs
be ensured without authorities intervening in ways which would
prevent resolution of the conflict by the parties?

Before turning in the next chapter to consider the resolution of
conflict, let us examine its nature. A gentleman was driving along a
narrow English country road and on approaching a bend was
confronted by an oncoming car which had swerved out on to his
track. At the last moment it pulled over to its correct side, marginally
avoiding tragedy. He noticed that there was an excited woman driver.
As she passed she called out 'Pig!' This appeared to add insult to near
injury, and he angrily responded, 'Cow!' He proceeded round the
corner and narrowly missed a pig. A few miles further on, reflecting
on the incident, he observed to himself, what a coincidence it was that
that cow of a driver had called him a pig, and that he had in fact
nearly run over a real pig! The predisposition of the gentleman to
perceive a female driver as incompetent, and therefore to attribute her
swerve to bad driving, the consequent misperception of her warning of
a pig on the road, and the failure of his own subsequent experience to
correct his misinterpretation of the warning, are typical of elements of
conflicts, regardless of their context: individual, small group, matrimonial, industrial or inter-state. Conflict at all social levels has similar
features. Regrettably, the world of knowledge has been split up into a
series of separate studies. There are the various natural sciences, and
there are many behavioural sciences such as psychology, anthropology, economics and politics. Indeed, there are specializations
within these, such as management studies. As part of this fragmenta-
tion of knowledge conflict at different social levels and in different
social contexts has been studied separately. The study of conflict in
industry, for example, derives little from its study elsewhere. Within
universities and training institutions generally it is at present fashion-
able to refer to 'interdisciplinary' approaches. But there is little
evidence that the psychologist does or even could communicate with
his colleagues in politics, or even reads outside his own make-believe
world. There is even less evidence that the manager or trade unionist
concerned with industrial conflict is aware of relevant knowledge and
experience among social caseworkers, mediators concerned with race
and communal relations, or others who have had experience at the
inter-state level.

There may be an approach to conflict, which is concerned with
conflict generally, that is more effective than an approach to conflict

at some particular level of interest. The following propositions emerged as the result of a research project in which parties to international conflicts were brought together into a face-to-face relationship.[54]

First, any one situation of conflict has many components, and in resolution it is necessary to break down the whole into its separate parties and issues. What appears at first sight to be a conflict between A and B over some one issue is usually a complex set of conflicts among many different factions and over a variety of issues. Those concerned with industrial dispute are aware of this aspect – even though the public image of a dispute may be one between A and B over wages.

Second, parties in an international conflict do not act irrationally, however 'irrational' their behaviour may appear to be: they respond to their environment in the way that appears to them to be most appropriate in the light of their perceptions of their environment, their goals and their costing of attainment of these goals. Industrial mediators can attest that this is so also in industrial conflict.

Third, international conflict is essentially a subjective relationship, dependent on sets of values and subjective perceptions of the motivations of the other side, even though it appears to the parties to be a conflict over an objective situation. In practice there is rarely, if ever, a cake of given size to be shared: the outcome of conflict can usually be positive sum – both parties can gain. This is probably a proposition with a general application.

Fourth, coercive or third-party settlements are rarely successful or stable; international conflict needs to be resolved and not just settled, and this means the need for processes by which the parties themselves determine the outcome. This is a departure from traditional notions of judicial settlement and third-party judgements, and it is as important at the international level as it is at the marital level, and one suspects, at the industrial level. There is a problem here. Fighting is a form of direct communication, and there is no reason to believe that direct negotiation between parties could lead to anything but a kind of fighting, as is evident in the Paris talks on Vietnam. Yet a decision or suggestion by a third party is likely to be irrelevant or an unacceptable compromise. The objective must be to transform the conflict from a confrontation to a problem-solving exercise. Direct face-to-face communication can be 'controlled' and transformed in this way by a different third-party activity. As we shall see, the role of the third party is to inject into the communication knowledge about the nature of conflict generally, the problems of perception, the processes of escalation, the confusion between role behaviour and personality, the errors in costing objectives and other aspects of it.

Fifth, the effective mediator at the small group, the international level and all levels between is the trained and experienced professional whose authority, like the authority of a doctor or any other professional, is based, not on his official role or backing, but on his professional skill. There is now a body of theory and experience, and there are results of experiments which offer effective means of resolving conflicts. At the same time, there are severe criticisms of most traditionally accepted explanations of conflict and means of resolving it. The ability reliably to resolve conflicts is a teachable skill.

Yet another proposition that has a general application is that even though face-to-face communication between nominees of parties can lead to an agreed resolution of conflict, the implementation of this agreement still poses a major problem. The difficult dispute to be resolved by controlled communication can be the consequent dispute between representatives and those they endeavour to represent. This raises issues regarding legitimization of leadership and representation, and these must be regarded as being within the area of concern to the mediator. Indeed, it is a futile exercise to resolve a conflict at one level if conflicts exists between that level and ones below.

Sufficient has been said to suggest that there are many aspects of conflict, both in its origins and its resolution, which are common to all kinds of social activity, whether they be the individual and his behaviour in society, marital relations, small-group relations, industrial relations or inter-state behaviour. The techniques of resolution of conflict at any one level are likely to be applicable at others: there is a common theoretical base.

How are we to ensure that community needs are met without interference with the processes of conflict resolution by the parties? The wider society cannot usefully force on parties a settlement of their disputes. The processes of resolution must acknowledge the parties as the principal actors. The interests of the wider community are interests to be taken into account by the parties. This is as true when two Cypriot parties are negotiating and touching upon the interests of Greece and Turkey, as it is when management and labour touch upon the interests of consumers. In practice the insertion of a community interest into a factional dispute usually increases, and does not decrease, the opportunities for effective resolution of the basic conflict. The ambitions of management for increased investment is in conflict with demands for increased wages. The resolution of this conflict is probably assisted by an assessment of community interest, for example, whether or not increased investment elsewhere should be promoted by the increased spending power of wage earners. Or to take another example, boredom originating on the shop floor cannot be eliminated by higher wages, shorter hours and increased leisure in a boring social environment. By relating work life to social life, by relating increased productivity to an improved social environment, there is a wider framework in which to tackle this problem to the advantage of industry and society. Local authorities are probably parties to a boredom conflict.

The general thesis that conflict and its resolution have features in common at all social levels has some institutional implications. Should there be organizations for the study and management of conflict confined to particular social levels, for example, should there be institutions or people who confine themselves to industrial or international conflict, or would better results be achieved if the approach were more broadly based so that experience at one level would feed into experience at others?

This is not merely an interesting academic question. It raises quite fundamental issues. There may be no such thing as international conflict which is not, in effect, the spill-over of an internal conflict within a state. The Second World War had its origins in stress conditions in Germany. French Indo-China wars were the direct outcome of the typically post-war Asian conflict between those who were endeavouring to maintain, and those who were endeavouring to eliminate, traditional feudal structures. Both factions sought outside assistance.

There is a corollary. States which experience external threat to their institutions tend to be those in which there is internal threat, and states which are secure internally have little to fear from external influence or subversion. The United States is heavily involved in many theatres of the world, not because it has a legitimate great power police role, or a duty to maintain the 'free world', but because many of its own institutions are felt to be under internal threat, as were the same institutions of Chiang Kai-shek's China, South Korea, the Philippines, Vietnam, the countries of Central and South America and elsewhere. The almost paranoiac 'fear' of communism in the United States arises out of a sense of insecurity due to the increasing inefficiency of some of its own institutions and decision-making processes, and to the social irrelevance of such institutions as corruption and special privilege. The general absence of such fears in Britain, for example, is due to a high level of shared values, and the widespread support for and confidence in the flexibility of its basic institutions.

If this reasoning is valid, it follows that the way in which international conflict can be avoided is the effective resolution of internal conflict. This is not to imply that there should be internally the maintenance of existing institutions or the resolution of conflict by authoritarian imposition of settlements. On the contrary, the effective resolution of conflict requires continuing change and outcomes of conflicts freely acceptable to the parties concerned, and to the wider community.

Conflict is symptomatic of change and altering values. There are those who derive satisfaction from promoting and aggravating conflict, and such people do not necessarily accept responsibility for finding solutions. There are those who call for 'law and order' and who seek to suppress conflict, and such people do not necessarily accept responsibility for the wider consequences of their actions, and the loss of some of the values they seek to preserve. These two factions, those promoting and those seeking to suppress conflict, left to themselves create conditions for 'isms', left and right.

Most states have gigantic institutions concerned with defence; but they merely toy with the problem of resolving conflicts in their societies which if left unresolved, could weaken from within those values and institutions that are widely supported in the community. Conflict is not a phenomenon that can be broken down to various levels of social behaviour, and attempts to resolve it should not be made separately at any particular level. Experience in one theatre can feed back into others. Furthermore, what appears to be conflict at one level, for example, the racial, in fact could originate out of conflict at another, for example, the industrial.

(ii) Fixed and variable sum outcomes

This view of the nature of conflict contains within it some major assumptions which have not been widely accepted in the past. For example, fundamental to popular thinking about inter-state relations has been the view that there is a fixed amount of satisfactions to be shared in any given set of inter-state relations. This view is deeply ingrained in popular political thinking. In this view the outcome of conflict must be such that any gain in satisfactions by one party to a dispute results in some loss to the other. It follows that conflict can be ended only by victory by one side and an ability to impose its terms on the other, by compromises made between the parties perhaps with the help of a mediator, by acceptance of third party decisions, or by third party enforcement of some conditions of settlement.

This pattern of classical political thought is essentially identical with economic thinking which postulated that economics is the study of the use of scarce resources in the satisfaction of infinite demands. In accordance with this frame of reference, for a state to be independent and secure it is necessary to have strategic materials under its control, to have alternative sources of supply, to have the physical means of taking resources if they are withheld, or to have an ideology that enables it to do without them. It is in this framework that we have been accustomed to thinking about the sovereign state in world society. In this competitive and power framework conflict is clearly 'objective' – meaning that two parties cannot have the same control over resources. It is in this framework that lawyers and mediators are asked to determine what division or settlement is 'just' and in accord with past rules and practices.

There seems to be no political equivalent of another economic model, that is the model provided by the theory of comparative costs. However, clearly there are integrative influences in relations between states, in addition to the disintegrative and defensive postures of the power model.

The point within the independence/integrative spectrum at which actors believe their relationships to be, depends on their perceptions of their relationships. Japan, before the war, required certain sources of raw materials and markets for its development. It endeavoured to obtain these within a commercial framework, presumably because it perceived its relationships with Britain and other Western trading partners as integrative. Tested against reality it became clear that it had misperceived its relationships: it had misjudged the consequences of the Great Depression. It then perceived its relationships as being towards the independence or power end of the spectrum. It acted accordingly and endeavoured to obtain by force a 'co-prosperity sphere' under its own control. Now, in the post war period, it perceives its relationships with independent Asian states as being integrative.

These perceptions were probably accurate: there were changes with changing conditions and after experience with reality. In the more typical case perceptions are not accurate and there are few opportunities for reality testing. Turkish Cypriot perceptions that Greek

Cypriots did not seek Cypriot independence and favoured Enosis proved to be false. The parties in the Middle East are certain that they have an accurate perception of the motivations of each other, while this seems far from certain to third parties. Perceptions by one party based on communications meant for different audiences, which are the usual source of perceptions, are frequently distorted.

This subjective element of perception in relationships is accompanied by another, namely the assessment of values sought in relation to costs. It is irrefutable that at a point of time conflict is 'objective'. At a point of time there are, by definition, incompatible goals, or competition for the occupancy of one or scarce positions. But no goal is unalterable. Goal changing is a process associated with conflict, especially as costs of attainment increase. New justifications are found for the continuation of policies that have failed to attain their original objectives. The United States perceived nationalist movements and attacks on certain indigenous types of land organization in Asia as a threat to its national interests. The initial estimate of costs of containing these attacks in terms of loss of goodwill internationally and domestically were acceptable. Additional information and reality testing of the motivations of the opposition and rising costs transformed the conflict from one in which the enemy's gain was perceived as the United States' loss, to one in which there could be positive gains from terminating conflict. Such an alteration in policy over time could be due only to subjective elements, that is, to reassessments of values in relation to costs.

This is probably typical of the course of conflict. The question arises whether there was initially an 'objective' conflict of interests other than the conflict at one point of time that was not affected by any cost assessments or other influences operating outside that one point of time. If not, to what extent was this initial awareness of conflict due to false perceptions of the motivations of the other party, and to false forecasting of costs (including false assessments of strength of feeling on the other side) in relation to values sought?

In short, while we have been conditioned by economic or sharing models, they are not necessarily relevant. In politics we are not dealing with scarcity. In politics we are dealing with security, independence and other values that increase in distributable size the more each actor has of them. A's perceived security or independence leads to policies that increase B's perceived security and independence. Conversely, when A perceives insecurity and adopts defensive postures, B senses insecurity: the total insecurity increases.

There is, therefore, the possibility that in any situation of conflict there are latent opportunities for sharing new options and of increasing satisfactions to be divided, as when resources can be exploited in common, and when security can be sought by mutual understanding. Accordingly, the outcome of resolution of conflict could be such that both sides could gain satisfactions, or both between them could share gains on a scale not possible if conflict continued. In such conditions a conflict could be ended by processes designed to lead parties to discover additional options and satisfactions in peaceful relations. A conflict that appears to be over 'objective' differences of interest, could be transformed into one that had a positive outcome for both parties, provided that the parties so reperceived each other that they could cooperate on a functional basis in the exploitation of the disputed resource. The mutual perception of motivations, however, determines whether the relationship is defensive ór could be integrative.

Admittedly there is an important interest element involved in any initial assessment of costs. British imperialism was probably a loss to Britain, but at the time it resulted in tremendous gains to some English. It is for this reason that an important part of the analysis of any conflict is an analysis of parties and issues. There cannot be resolution of conflict at one systems level in the absence of resolution at lower levels. Frequently resolution of inter-state conflict must commence within the state parties. Conflict is 'objective' only in relation to the interest elements involved.

This interest element turns out to be time element. Conflict with Japan was far less due to Japanese miscalculations than to British ones. The textile and related interests were threatened immediately. The long-term costs of depression policies to the interests concerned, and to the wider public, were not calculated.

There is another meaning of 'objective' conflict. The power struggle to secure positions of independence creates institutional and structural conditions which are themselves 'objective' conditions. Conflict that takes place within these conditions, or which is designed to alter them, must be treated as 'objective'. Actor *A* (Greek Cypriots), in a privileged position, is not likely to forego his position unless confronted by actor *B* (Turkish Cypriots) who is in an underprivileged position. Both perceive their relationship accurately – no reperception would remove the 'objective' conditions. This is, however, not a special case: it is a case in which the interest and time factors happen to be particularly important. The conflict in Vietnam was an 'objective' one: interest groups endeavoured to maintain existing agricultural systems and institutions of privilege, and believed that they could do so. In South Africa and Rhodesia the position is the same. Rarely are persons in privileged positions willing to look ahead more than two generations. Defensive or holding tactics are pursued. It is not until costs are clear and have to be met immediately that they are taken into account. This has been true in industrial relations. These extreme cases do not, however, invalidate the general proposition that conflicts are subjective – even the 'objective' conditions are subjective in the sense that their maintenance presents costs and ultimately the sacrifice of values of even greater importance. If this were not so slavery and feudalism would still be widespread. The question is whether the processes of costing can be accelerated.

Nor is the 'objective contradiction' said to be inherent in relations between socialist and capitalist states a special case. If one were to predict mutual convergence under social and technological pressures, the problem would be defined away in the long term – and there is some empirical evidence in support of this. But even though this were not assumed, the contradictions do not necessarily produce conflict unless it is also assumed that all other values are subordinated to the preservation of these systems. Goal changing and shifts in priorities occur with environmental changes. In a thermonuclear world, and moreover, one in which fundamental challenges are being made to all forms of authority that do not provide reciprocal benefits, what appear now to be basic contradictions between socialism and capitalism could vanish into thin air as costing of values becomes more realistic. A privileged/underprivileged or North/South conflict could prove to be more basic. And the consequences of this conflict would then require costing.

In arguing that conditions of conflict are subjective, one is not arguing that there always exist conditions of possible integration. There are conditions of political development without which there cannot be internal integration, and therefore, integration with another political unit. These include an ability to overcome environmental restraints in the achievement of goals; ability to change priorities of political actors; ability to change occupiers of roles; and ability to alter roles and structure of offices. The absence of these conditions is in itself a cause of conflict or latent conflict, and even ad hoc functional cooperation becomes difficult. However, this is merely another way of stating the hypothesis that resolution of conflict is possible only between integrated units. Attempts to resolve conflict must frequently commence, therefore, at systems levels below the inter-state one.

The image of world society as comprising states as separate entities promotes the notion of objective conflict. In practice in conflicts there are few definable state 'interests', but many interests held in common by factions in different states. It is for this reason that internal conflict spills over to create international conflict. This becomes clear when parties and issues are defined and isolated. Greek and Turkish Cypriots have been divided within themselves, each faction finding supporters in Greece and Turkey or elsewhere. Furthermore, there appear to be values, such as independence, which are widely if not universally held. World society (not necessarily represented by states or the United Nations) exercises its influence on authorities that seek to deny these values in preserving their own interests. Press, radio, publications, non-governmental institutions help to create the environment in which state authorities act. Authorities are ultimately required to assess the costs involved in resisting political demands made on them.

Nor can it be assumed that the values at stake are primarily material. African leaders have claimed that independence is to be preferred to law and order, and material progress. Opportunities to travel, to read scientific literature, to learn of conditions abroad, to be educated, to have equality of opportunities of all kinds, to participate in decisions affecting the environment, are values widely held by people generally and by some governments. It is these which come to the surface when conflict is being analysed. The declared reasons for conflict are often merely symbols, as when frustration and monotony lead factory workers to strike over hours or the conditions of changing rooms.

In summary, in any interaction of systems there are conflicts in objectives; but objectives involve preferences, and preferences can change. Consequently, relationships within a situation of conflict can change, and there are, therefore, possible forms of resolution from which both parties can gain. There are also subjective influences involved in the different perceptions parties have of each other and of the world environment, and in the consideration they give to the costs of conflict involved in delaying settlements. Conflict can be transformed from violence and coercion into a problem-solving exercise with a positively beneficial result once there are opportunities to test perceptions and to assess costs of conflict in relation to values being pursued. Arbitration and mediation allow them to remain as 'objective' conditions, and sources of conflict in the future. Perhaps we have argued too much about political conditions when we should be looking more at the technique and its effectiveness in dealing with them. What we should be exploring is whether conflict which is perceived as having a gain or loss outcome can be transformed into conflict that appears to have a positive outcome for all parties by re-examination of perceptions, goals and costs.

11. *Resolution of conflict*

Now let us try to set down, step by step, the procedures that seem to be required in the resolution of a communal or inter-state conflict – or, indeed, any conflict – and to give the theoretical reasons for each.

This third part of our study has been called 'Prescription' because we have moved from an analysis of world society to applied social science. Our concern with dysfunctional conflict is a concern with how to prevent it, or to resolve it when it has occurred. In some ways this is a departure from traditional studies. We are not concerned merely with the absence of war, that is a peace kept by threat, collective security or nuclear deterrence. This has been the main concern of scholars and politicians. We are now looking for means of dealing with conflict so that there can be a self-supporting condition of peace. This means that we are making a distinction between the 'settlement' and the 'resolution' of conflict, that is, a distinction between an outcome determined by a third party and forced upon those in conflict, and an outcome acceptable to the parties which requires no enforcement.

(i) Traditional approaches to the settlement of conflict
There are three elements in the settlement or resolution of conflict: the degree of third-party coercive intervention, the degree of participation by the conflicting parties, and the degree of communication between the parties. The history of attempts to deal with conflicts shows a continuous decline in the degree of third-party coercion, and a continuous increase in both participation and communication between the parties. The implication is that there has been a continuous shift away from 'settlements' toward attempts at 'resolution'. But there has been, so far, as little success with resolution as there was with settlement. Let us see if we can find out why, and whether we can employ our previous analysis of world society to point to likely future trends.

Judicial settlements, that is a decision by a court based on precedence and considerations of justice, was, and still is, the most favoured means of dealing with a conflict. Scholars and politicians have repeatedly argued that, if only states would refer their disputes to the International Court, conflict could be avoided. But states have been reluctant to refer their disputes to the Court. Once entered upon, judicial procedures remove the ultimate power of decision from states, and in respect of disputes involving political considerations this is usually unacceptable to states. Not only is the power of decision removed; it is transferred to an authority whose responses cannot reliably be forecast and whose guidelines are sometimes far from clear, and when clear not always thought to be relevant. There is, in the case of judicial settlement, virtually no participation by the parties, and no direct communication.

Judicial settlements being unacceptable, the device of arbitration has been employed. Legal procedures are followed, and the finding is binding on the conflicting parties; but procedures can be more flexible. Furthermore, the parties participate at least to the extent that usually each nominates an arbitrator. Nevertheless, the process suffers from the drawbacks of judicial settlement: final decision-making responsibility is removed from the parties concerned.

Mediation is a convenient form when the parties do not feel themselves free to communicate directly. There is a high degree of participation by the parties, but communication between them remains ineffective. There are inherent difficulties in mediation, particularly when the parties are not brought into face-to-face contact. When the mediator endeavours to represent to one party the views of the other, he tends to be identified by each party with the interests of the other. An explanation of the behaviour of the other party is treated as sympathy with that party. He soon becomes regarded by both with suspicion. Parties in conflict cannot accept neutral positions: 'if you are not with us you are against us' is a common attitude. The longer mediation continues the less, and not the more, is the mediator likely to be accepted as disinterested and unprejudiced.

Conciliation is more directed toward activities designed to help parties to agreement, and there can be a high degree of participation and communication. Provided there are no commitments in advance, this process does not infringe the right of parties to accept or to reject any proposals. However, in practice there are generally some implied obligations to reach some conclusion, and parties involved in conflict are not always free to enter even into this process.

'Negotiation' is a term differently used in different contexts. Sometimes it is a generic term used to include all non-judicial and arbitral processes, such as conciliation and mediation. For reasons of clarity it is convenient to restrict the use of this term to exchanges that take place directly between the parties, that is, in the absence of third parties.

Negotiations of this direct type have an advantage over judicial processes because the whole of a relationship can be discussed, including political aspects. Furthermore, they can be held in secret. No third party suggests, influences or coerces, and the parties retain their independence of decision. Judicial processes and negotiations are two extremes: the one removes decision-making from the parties, and the other leaves it wholly with the parties.

There is no more frequently-employed means of controlling relationships between states than negotiation, and probably conflict avoidance sometimes results from it. However, negotiations of this direct type have a limited place in the peaceful settlement of disputes once they occur, especially once the level of conflict has escalated. There are many reasons for this. If direct contact is possible between parties in conflict, the probability is that one will be in a position to coerce the other, and a negotiated settlement is likely to lead to an agreement which creates conflict in the future. Peace settlements are negotiated in a victor-vanquished framework, and negotiation that avoids hostilities is no less within a power framework. Even compromise settlements arrived at because the power relationship is not clear-cut, are likely to provide the origins of future conflict. There being no external source of information and experience, and no alternatives except those the parties themselves produce, the range of choice is limited. Having in mind the prejudices, images and stereotypes, suspicions and fears of parties involved in a conflict situation, the probability of further escalation of conflict during negotiation would be as high as conflict resolution. In practice, direct negotiation, which implies full participation and full communication between the parties, merely transfers the conflict from the battlefield to the conference table. Dropping bombs is one form of participation and communication in a conflict. Argument around the table is not necessarily a more effective form of communication.

Where do we go from here? We have a process which eliminates third-party coercion, and provides for participation and communication – and we are no nearer resolution of conflict.

(ii) Behavioural approaches to conflict resolution

We must turn back to our analysis. We have found that conflict is subjective, involving perceptions and values. We have found that it need not have win-lose outcomes. We have argued that objectives and values are held in common, and that functional cooperation is possible in achieving them. The problem of resolving conflict, whether at the inter-state, communal, industrial or any other level, is the problem of transforming a situation that appears to be a power bargaining or win-lose one, into a problem-solving one in which both sides can gain. This is the procedure frequently adopted in small group conflict and matrimonial conflict. Has it any application at the level of interest to us? Is what we are looking for a new role for the third party, one that is not coercive in any sense, that does not inhibit the participation and communication of the parties, but renders that communication so effective that problems of perception are overcome, and realistic assessments of costs of objectives sought are made?

The differences between traditional mediation in the international field, and the processes of conflict resolution that have been tested in the social field, are striking. Indeed, when means of resolving conflict within a society are applied to the international field they seem to turn traditional mediation on its head. 'Authority', which a traditional mediator might welcome and derive from the United Nations or from great power backing, would seem to a sociologist or a social caseworker to be undesirable except insofar as it was derived, as is the authority of a doctor, from a recognition by the parties of a professional experience. Or again, 'solutions' and 'compromises' are usually suggested by traditional mediators, whereas the caseworker would avoid making suggestions and would endeavour to stimulate the parties to arrive at these.

The following table may appear at first sight to present a caricature of attitudes of a traditional mediator; but the list was compiled during two different conferences at which mediators and professional diplomats were pooling their experiences. Alternatives, which depict the approach we have adopted, are given in the right-hand column.

1 Mediation is an art; there are 'born' mediators who cannot pass on their techniques; success is measured by the reputation of the mediator as diplomat or lawyer, and not by his performance for this is determined by the complexity of the situation.	Mediation is a learned technique and performance is measured by success and failure.

2 The personality of the mediator is the important consideration.

Personal temperament is relevant to all occupations; but the presence or absence of learned techniques is the important consideration.

3 'Time is the essence': at some stage, which cannot be defined, conflicts can be resolved, at others not.

Conditions in which conflict can or cannot be resolved can be determined: if 'time is the essence' then conflict is like the common cold and will cure itself, making the mediator irrelevant.

4 No two cases are the same: conflicts are like road accidents, they just happen.

There are common patterns in conflicts, making them essentially the same and subject to the same techniques.

5 The mediator requires power support, from an international institution, powerful states or financial institutions.

There is a difference between enforced settlement and resolution of conflict, and the latter is accomplished without support except respect for the professional knowledge and status of the mediator; authority is derived from the parties and not from external institutions.

6 It is the duty of the mediator to suggest solutions.

It is only the parties that can arrive at solutions, and the mediator should never prejudice his position by making them.

7 The mediator's genius is in suggesting reasonable and workable compromises.

No party should ever be asked to accept a compromise, and the mediation exercise is to arrive at alternative goals or means that do not require compromise.

8 The interests of greater powers and world society as a whole must sometimes be placed before the interests of the parties.

In any conflict the relations of the parties most directly concerned take precedence, and are then subjected to the resolution of any conflict they have with interests at other levels.

9 Relations between states are relations between authorities within them, and mediation must be between authorities involved in a conflict situation.

World society does not comprise states as separate entities but transactions of all kinds that cut state boundaries: mediation must be at different levels involving different parties and different issues, sometimes parties within parties, and not only legal authorities.

10 International conflict is separate from domestic conflict.

International conflict is usually a spill-over from domestic conflict in which parties seek foreign assistance, and mediation must involve domestic consideration of ethnic and other groups, and not be confined to international conflict.

11 States 'should' accept processes of arbitration and mediation.	No state can be expected to submit to third-party judgements, or be involved in processes which place it in a position of having to accept a consensus view. Failure to accept some form of arbitration or mediation is a reflection on the mediation process and is not evidence of a government's unwillingness to resolve the conflict or to cooperate in world society.
12 Some decision-makers behave 'irrationally'.	Parties to a conflict are responding to the situation in the way that appears most beneficial to them in the light of the knowledge they have of the motivations of others and the options open: 'irrational' behaviour is behaviour not understood or not approved by others.
13 No fixed procedures are possible.	A quite strict adherence to rules of procedure is desirable once they have been tested.
14 The mediator should be one person.	The mediator needs to be a panel of specialists in the field of conflict.

One could go on almost endlessly in this vein – at the risk of creating misunderstandings because of the nature of the short expositions on the right-hand side. But these are sufficient to make the point: rather than work from ascertained 'facts' in a particular situation, the third party needs to apply generalizations about conflict to the particular situation being examined, thereby helping to analyse it.

There is a hidden hypothesis here. If the role of the third party is confined to feeding in information about conflicts, and is not concerned with suggesting 'solutions' or arriving at assessments, there is an implied assumption that the analysis of a particular conflict, within this analytical framework, itself leads to the resolution of the conflict. There is a hypothesis that once the relationships have been analysed satisfactorily, once each side is accurately informed of the perceptions of the other, of the alternative values and goals, of the alternative means and costs of attaining them, there are outcomes acceptable to the parties. It is assumed, for instance, that some crucial misunderstandings will be revealed that will alter the relationship. In the Cyprus situation, the realization by the Turkish Cypriots that Greek Cypriots sought an independent Cyprus and not union with Greece, despite official statements to the contrary, could change the relationships of the communities and the nature of the problem to be solved. Greek and Turkish Cypriots could wage common cause against minority elements seeking Enosis, partition, and union with Turkey.

This hypothesis rests on another, that conflict is essentially subjective. The traditional view is, as we have seen, that while subjective elements are present, there is a dominating 'objective' conflict of interests. The traditional assumption is that there is a fixed amount of satisfactions to be shared in any given situation, a cake of given size to be divided in some proportion. The 'cake' need not be a physical property: it can be security, fear or a sphere of influence. Accordingly, in this view the conclusion of conflict must be such that any gain in satisfactions by one side results in an equal loss to the other. But there is the possibility, as we have seen, that in any situation of conflict the outcome could be such that both sides could gain satisfactions, or both between them could share gains on a scale not possible if conflict continued. A breakthrough would occur in the abilities of states to manage their inter-state relations if means were found to change the game from one in which fixed or negative outcomes were anticipated, to one in which the possibilities of positive outcome for all parties were perceived.

(iii) A theoretical framework

It follows from these remarks that a first step in approaching conflict, either to analyse it or to resolve it, is to be aware of the body of relevant theory and empirical work that is available, and the hypotheses and propositions that have been advanced and sometimes tested. This body of knowledge is extensive, and covers two areas of study, first the nature of world society, and second the nature of conflict. The relevance of the first is that it directs attention to propositions concerning structural causes of conflict, the consequences of social and political change, the spill-over of domestic conflict into international relations, and other phenomena of this kind. It also guides the parties and the third party in their consideration of outcomes, which, if they are to be effective in resolving the conflict, must conform with world trends and conditions. Not generally realized, perhaps, is the extent to which images of world society held by conflicting parties and mediators control their thinking and determine 'solutions'. In the case of an internal conflict in which one tribe wished to secede, an approach based on the nineteenth-century concepts of world society comprising legal entities would lead a traditional mediator to seek constitutional solutions designed to restore unity. An approach based on a contemporary systems model, and a knowledge of trends toward smaller political entities within larger economic units could lead to an acceptance of different outcomes. Or again, in a dispute over boundaries, like the Somalia-Kenya dispute, the traditional mediator would be concerned with the legal and historical 'facts' about the boundary, whereas within a systems framework the orderly control of transactions across the boundary would seem more relevant than the boundary itself, opening up a different set of possible outcomes. Theoretical literature also directs attention to universal behavioural responses that are relevant to all disputes: social-psychological values attached to participation, independence, equality of opportunity and others that are emerging in university campus conflicts no less than in communal and inter-state conflicts.

The relevance of the literature on conflict is more apparent, but it is doubtful whether traditional mediation has taken sufficiently into account the results of experiment and experience in the handling of individual, small group and industrial conflict. There are hypotheses and propositions in the literature of conflict and integration that help in giving alternative perspectives to conflict at the inter-state level.[55]

(iv) Parties or systems levels

Historians, journalists and observers generally tend to report on communal and inter-state conflicts as total situations in which two parties are aligned against each other. The last war was between the 'Allies' and the 'Nazi' and 'Fascist powers'. The Middle East conflict was reported as being between Israel and Arab States. The communal conflict in Ireland was described in terms of Catholics and Protestants. The Security Council took decisions about the Cyprus problem as though it were one situation, naming Greece, Turkey, the two Cypriot communities and the United Kingdom as being concerned.

In every conflict, however, there are a great many 'parties' at different levels of political organization. Each has different interests in the conflict. The desire to resolve conflict at one level, and an actual agreement, do not necessarily resolve the conflict. In a London strike the union representatives of rubbish collectors reached an agreement, but workers in various localities continued to strike. Agreement between Greece and Turkey would not necessarily resolve the Cyprus problem, and agreement between Egypt and Israel on the Canal and other matters of common concern would not solve the Middle East problem which is directly related to the interests of Palestinians.

The consideration of political levels is more important than appears at first sight. It has become even more important in recent years because peoples are now insisting upon participation in decision-making that affects them. Maybe it was once possible for greater powers, or the dominant parties to a dispute, to coerce others into an agreement, or for a third party to impose a settlement. It is not so now. There are communal tensions and differences in every mixed village in Cyprus stemming from religious beliefs, educational systems and traditional attitudes of inferiority or superiority that cannot be eliminated by some overall agreement reached at an inter-state political level. In Ireland agreement between the governments of Northern Ireland and Westminster did not stop fighting in the streets. Resolution of conflict rests, finally, upon agreements at those levels most affected by the conflict, that is, the levels at which conflict damages or severs the mass of transactions between peoples.

There are different issues at stake at different political levels. There is never one set of 'war aims'. In the Cyprus situation Greece and Turkey have interests which relate to their own domestic and bilateral interests; the Greek and Turkish communities have a different set of fears and ambitions; there are conflicts within each community; there are special relations between Turks and Turkey, and Greeks and Greece; there are issues at stake among the USA, Greece and Turkey; the UK has special interests, some of which are in conflict with Cypriot interests. No mediation proposals are likely to satisfy all. Those who believe that conflict can be settled by greater powers imposing their will upon others would argue that the interested parties first to be involved are the greater powers. The inclusion of Greece, Turkey and the United Kingdom in the Security Council Resolution which made possible the appointment of a mediator is evidence of the presence of this approach. The great power discussions on the Middle East conflict are further evidence. If, on the other hand, it is argued that resolution of conflict and a stable condition of peace can be achieved only by treating it at source, then parties at more local political levels would be regarded as those first to be involved in mediation.

A logically related proposition is that agreement reached at local and more intense levels of political and other transactions would necessarily be acceptable – with minor modifications to cater for special interests – at other levels. In Cyprus agreement between the communities is a prerequisite for resolution of the communal conflict and a solution acceptable to Greece and Turkey. In the Middle East agreement between Israel and Palestinians will be acceptable to Arab states, which will then be in a position to arrive at agreements specifically on those other issues which involve them.

The typical situation of conflict is even more conflictual, and a starting point in the analysis and resolution of conflict is often within each of the parties involved. In Northern Ireland 'the parties' comprise many different viewpoints. Unless each party can be identified, unless representative views and aims can be determined, there is no possibility of mediation in any form. Ultimately persons, legitimized (not necessarily legal) authorities, representing parties must be identified.

Consequently, the second step, having examined theoretical and empirical studies of conflict and the world society in which it takes place, is to identify the parties at their various political levels, and the issues that are in dispute in each case.

(v) The mediator

An important principle of mediation is that the only source of information is the parties concerned. Conflict, like all relationships, is a perceived relationship. What is of interest to the third party is what is perceived by the conflicting parties. Indeed, the less, and not the more, the third party knows in advance of the 'facts' of the situation to be approached, the better. He does not then project his own viewpoints, or select data and make assessments on the basis of his own experiences and prejudices. This view is expanded below. Despite this, however, some preliminary enquiries are required. It is necessary to determine the general structural framework as a guide to the type of hypothesis which is relevant (that is, the area of theoretical literature which is relevant), and the type of person or persons who are relevant as a third party.

The nature of a behavioural approach draws attention to the need for the third party to be a panel and not a single mediator. First, there is a wide range of specialized knowledge and experience necessary, and this cannot be within the competence of one person. Second, the approach is not the fact finding normative one of the traditional mediator which seeks to arrive at a reasonable 'settlement' or compromise, perhaps leaving the origins of the dispute untouched. It is not a bargaining exercise, but a problem-solving one. The aim is, as explained above, to transform the outcome of conflict from a cake-dividing one in which the gain of one side is the loss of the other, into an outcome in which both sides can claim attainment of their immediate minimum objectives, and, by functional cooperation, perhaps both gain by the outcome in the longer term. A panel is appropriate in such a problem-solving exercise, and indeed, almost a seminar discussion in which the parties are members with the same objectives and status as the third party.

The 'experts' required on a panel are those who are aware of the nature of conflict and the common patterns that appear, and not those who know the situation in detail, and who have already made up their minds that the conflict is due to the personality of a leader, to the character of a people, to historical antagonisms and other factors that feature in typical accounts of conflict. Conflicts are characterized by common patterns of behaviour on the part of the parties – their attitudes to each other, their fears, their interpretations of events. There are many aspects of a conflict that can be analysed reliably by those without knowledge of the geographical, historical, institutional and other structural and environmental features. Indeed, such knowledge probably does no more than attract attention to some superficial differences between conflicts. There are common patterns of behaviour and common sequences in the development of escalation of conflicts. The purpose of discussion is, furthermore, to assist the parties in testing their perceptions of the situation against reality. It is they that determine the 'facts' that are relevant, within a theoretical framework that ensures that sensitive and apparently irrelevant influences are not omitted. The regional expert could destroy the nature of the approach. So, too, could the lawyer, or any one with an ideology or sets of norms who would be inclined to depart from the supportive role of the third party. The behaviour of the parties is not judged by any set of norms. It is accepted as the most appropriate response to the environment of which the party is capable within the limits of its perceptions, knowledge and goals. While traditional mediation has usually been regarded as having a judicial aspect, and while lawyers have frequently been selected as mediators, a different type of specialist is required by this approach.

Specialization is not the only, or even the most important qualification of a panel member. There are temperamental factors. There are probably few more sensitive situations than ones in which parties to a violent dispute are brought face to face with each other in the presence of a third party, or even just separately with a third party. An ability to identify with the party, that is to adopt what the caseworker would call a 'supportive' approach, is essential. To a large degree this is training as much as temperament. If someone is trained within a systems framework and understands systems response to the environment, it is easier to adopt the position that every party in a dispute is responding in the best way it can to achieve its goals, in the light of its knowledge of the environment, its perceptions of the other party, the options available, the restraints on its own decision-making, and other influences of this order. Moral and normative judgements are not then relevant. Furthermore, if the role of the third party is confined to injecting information about conflict, which it is argued here it should be, the consequences of third-party prejudice and temperament are reduced.

(vi) Face-to-face discussion

There have been many occasions on which a mediator has found it impossible to bring the parties into a face-to-face situation. The reasons are never clear, and usually an impression is conveyed that one side or the other is being difficult, irrational, uncooperative or unreasonable. But the reasons are usually sound ones from the point of view of the parties. In the Cypriot case each side was attempting to promote a particular interpretation of a constitutional position: each side would meet only in conditions which satisfied its interpretation. This was because mediation was perceived essentially as a bargaining process, and neither side was prepared to prejudice its position by appearing to accept the position of the other. In the Middle East case the UAR refused to meet Israel in what would be perceived as a face-to-face victor-vanquished relationship. Furthermore, events made it clear that the UAR, though perceived by Israel as the opposing party, was no more a party than Greece and Turkey were parties to the Cyprus dispute. The 'parties' were in this case Israel and the Palestinians. Face-to-face discussions between them would be meaningful, whereas face-to-face discussions with Arab states would be not unlike face-to-face discussions with an agent of the party principally involved.

As a general principle it can be set down that mediation should not take place unless there is face-to-face communication between the parties in the presence of the mediator. Refusal is a warning light that the parties have not been identified correctly, that the mediation framework is not appropriate, or that some other precondition to an effective mediation is missing. The likelihood is that mediation would fail if the parties were coerced into meeting, and that mediation by discussions with the parties separately will fail.

Furthermore, there is a specific reason why a mediator should not see parties separately. There is a strong 'if you are not with us, you are against us' outlook among parties involved in a dispute. Even a report and interpretation of the position of the other side by the mediator is likely to be treated as demonstrating a hostile or prejudiced approach by the parties. In due course the mediator comes to be treated just with diplomatic courtesy.

The next stage is discussion. The way in which this is conducted depends on the approach being adopted. If the approach is that of King Solomon, the third party will quickly give his view on the basis of his idea of a reasonable and just solution. If it is the approach of the traditional mediator, the third party will endeavour to persuade the parties to negotiate, that is bargain, with his proposed solution as a starting point. With a behavioural approach the processes would be designed to avoid a bargaining framework, to avoid suggested 'solutions' and compromises, and to create conditions in which the conflict could be analysed to show its origins, its escalation, the motivations of the parties, the differences between motivations and perceived motivations, alternative means of attaining objectives and matters of these kinds.

As has already been suggested, analysis and resolution of conflict, within this framework, are one and the same thing. It is the analysis that is seminal, not the insights of the third party. Once both parties are able to understand, if not identify with, the problems faced by the other, the analysis is complete, and consideration is then given to alternative means of achieving objectives. This usually involves areas of functional cooperation. It is to this end that discussions are directed.

The promotion of functional cooperation is the positive step to be taken by the third party once analysis is complete, once, that is, the conditions are favourable to a functional approach. It is not sufficient for the third party merely to leave the parties to get on with it. Their relationships are still influenced by mutual distrust and memories of past behavioural patterns that trigger off hostile responses. There is, furthermore, an absence of consolidated machinery for consultation. The role of the third party does not cease after analysis is complete, and controlled communication is established: this is merely the precondition for activities through which new relationships and institutions emerge. The important consideration is to avoid constitutional or institutional 'solutions', and allow these to evolve over a period of time within a framework of functional cooperation.

(vii) Assessment
'An introduction to the study of international relations in our time is an introduction to the art and science of the survival of mankind.'

This is an observation made by Karl Deutsch to whom reference has already been made. What has been suggested in this study is that world society is a unity, the study is man, and for this reason we need to study conflict in world society at all levels. World society and its problems are not 'over there' – remote from us. We live and work within it. The nature of conflict, and the ways in which it can be handled are similar at domestic, communal and inter-state levels, and experience at any one level is helpful at others. It is a problem everyone can think about, and everyone can experiment with.

12. *Concluding observations and a simulation exercise*

We commenced this examination of world society with an analysis of relations among states, and the transactions within the whole world society. We finally tested this by applying the analysis to the most important problem – the one which leads us to be interested in a study of world society – the problem of conflict and its resolution.

What has emerged is a view, an approach, a set of hypotheses and prescriptive proposals that might appear novel and even controversial if they were not a reflection of our everyday experience within our own personal social relationships. Every aspect of behaviour in world society – role behaviour, decision-making, 'non-rational' behaviour, the problems of perceptions, values, the spill-over of conflict, supportive approaches to conflict – relate directly to what we know by experience of behaviour in all social groups. Behaviour in world society by states, institutions and people necessarily relates to behaviour in more confined areas: any artificial separation of politics from international politics, or any approach to an understanding of world society that implies one set of theories to explain behaviour at one social level, and another set at another level, must be misleading. There will never be a 'one world' in an institutional sense; but there is one world in a behavioural sense. Furthermore, we will understand behaviour of states, of groups within states, and of men if we place them in the broader framework of world society.

This has been essentially a simple analysis, but not a simplified one. It is one with which we can experiment. In our everyday life we can observe 'role behaviour', whether deterrence deters, whether authority is legitimized. From morning to night we can be 'testing' hypotheses concerning behaviour.

It is instructive deliberately to 'simulate' behaviour in world society. This can be done very simply by twenty or so people forming into groups of four or five, each enacting the behaviour of states and factions within them, and each person enacting a particular role within either the public or the private sector. Below is an outline of a simulation exercise.

It is possible to 'simulate' a crisis situation, for example, the Middle East. But there are inherent disadvantages in this because the actors enact the roles of the persons involved, and endeavour to adopt their basic prejudices, misperceptions and assumptions. It is more instructive to simulate a situation in a way which makes possible exploration of alternative behaviour, and in this way try to discover whether or not these prejudices, misperceptions and assumptions are an integral part of behaviour in world society. Such a situation is an imaginary one of a world of four or five states with no previous relations, and only certain physical characteristics. It is interesting that young students, army officers and decision-makers who have nothing but conventional wisdom to guide them soon face crises and conflicts in such a simulation exercise. Students who have been taught to be analytical and to avoid self-defeating policies avoid a power confrontation, and embark upon integrative processes. The simulation game is, as a consequence, far less exciting, but gives far more insight into the nature of relationships, and why they are so frequently conflictual.

The following is a report of a typical simulation exercise given to first-year university students at the end of their course, the purpose being to provide an opportunity to apply the knowledge they had gained in an interacting situation. (It would be quite instructive to give the same simulation before and after the course so that students could compare their behaviour on the basis of their conventional wisdom with their behaviour at the end of the course.)

As a preliminary, students were given a questionnaire designed to persuade them to place themselves in the shoes of decision-makers in other states – designed, that is, to offset as far as possible their national outlooks. They were asked twenty questions such as, 'If you were the Government of South Africa, would you pursue a policy of apartheid?', 'If you were the Government of Sweden, would you opt for nuclear weapons?'. After questionnaires were completed, the results were discussed. The habit of identifying with the country being enacted in simulation is a necessary prerequisite, especially when so many students enter courses with single-solution ideas, and preconceived notions about world affairs.

The next step was to distribute copies of an outline of the

simulation exercise to be undertaken, including a map of the imaginary world to be simulated. This outline gave basic information respecting each of five states, and the general arrangements of the exercise.

'Simulation exercise'

The situation to be simulated is an imagined one: the world comprises only five states, each with certain characteristics which resemble certain states in the South East Asia and Pacific area. Each is described below.

The world environment in which they exist is the present one, that is the technological, specialization, trading and cultural levels are contemporary ones. At the outset of the run there are no alliances, and no overt conflicts in process. Each state recognizes and has normal relations with others. The force capabilities of the states indicate that some are more fearful or more expansionist than others – there is no widespread harmony.

Each state will be manned by three actors, a domestic and a foreign decision-maker, and a leader. In the event of anyone not present to act, internal arrangements can be made; but if there is disagreement on a major issue and the leader is opposed, the government falls and roles must be changed. If numbers permit, there should be a leader of an opposition, and/or a representative of some faction within the community.

The policy objectives of each state and its general character will be determined by the actors. In preparation all actors are expected to make a study of the policies of states that are typical of those they are to simulate. They are required to identify with them as good actors on the stage identify with the roles they play.

Any communication to another state, or public communication to all states, must be written and given to the communications officer for distribution.

From time to time the run will be halted and actors will be asked to introspect and explain their last decision. In expectation of this, notes should be taken of all negotiations and decisions.

From time to time also, as may seem required, all actors will come together to form an international institution of the General Assembly type.

Rules will be introduced as the run proceeds: in the main these should arise out of relations that develop and not be determined in advance.

The states are: Lusitania; Mauretania; Dacia; Numidia; Aquitania.

They are positioned as shown in Fig. 15, and their features are described below:

Lusitania. A state with a large area, plus a vast expanding and illiterate population resisting efforts at birth control. The economy is predominantly a peasant one, run on a subsistence basis. Some undeveloped natural resources, plus a few infant industries. Great dependence upon foreign aid for capital creation; very slow rate of economic growth.

Basic capability 15,000; force capability 700; minimum consumption satisfaction 10,000; decision latitude 8.

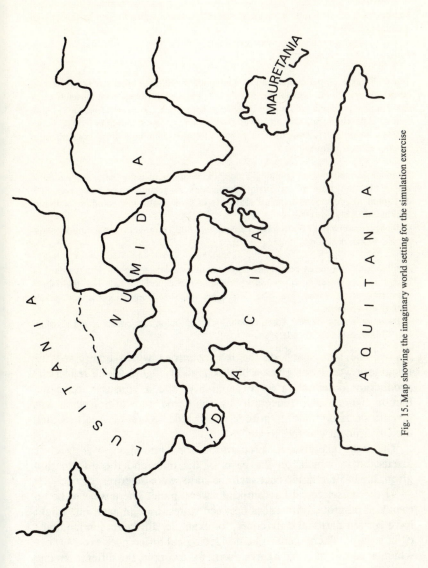

Fig. 15. Map showing the imaginary world setting for the simulation exercise

Mauretania. Small area; position of 'off-shore' island. Large population though rate of growth slowing slightly. Highly industrialized with a need for overseas markets and sources of raw material. Very high rate of economic growth and a fairly high standard of living.

Basic capability 25,000; force capability 2,200; minimum consumption satisfaction 13,000; decision latitude 6.

Dacia. Weakly united confederation, scattered over a large area containing several ethnic groups. Small population, mostly still engaged in subsistence agriculture. A few primary products grown on a large scale on estates. Few natural resources, little industrial development, slow economic growth rate and low standard of living.

Basic capability 12,000; force capability 500; minimum consumption satisfaction 5,000; decision latitude 4.

Numidia. Large loose geographical area with no common centre; large population of several clashing ethnic groups, one predominating. Huge undeveloped resources, lack of capital for development hence slow rate of growth and low standard of living. Politically highly unstable.

Basic capability 17,000; force capability 1,800; minimum consumption satisfaction 9,000; decision latitude 5.

Aquitania. A large area containing a very small population with a high standard of living. Large producer of primary products for exports; small but flourishing industrial sector. Rapid rate of economic growth, slow population increase, stable form of government.

Basic capability 22,000; force capability 1,100; minimum consumption satisfaction 13,000; decision latitude 4.

As will be seen, each of the five countries which comprised the imaginary world was given a basic capability figure which reflects its production potential, a force capability, and a consumption satisfaction figure which reflects living standards. In addition each was given a decision-making latitude which reflected the degree to which the government was free to act.

The next exercise in preparation for simulation was a class discussion in which, on the basis of the map and the information given, the basic relations between the states were determined.

At the outset certain assumptions were made. There were to be no racial or religious differences between states, though each one might have certain national differences, for example, differences in language or in culture. There were to be no ideological differences except those which arise out of basic figures given, for example, the differences one would expect to find in underdeveloped and in developed states.

By examining only the information given, it was found that each of the states had certain characteristics and relations with other states.

Mauretania, the smallest of all the states geographically, had the highest basic capability, the highest force capability, and the highest consumption satisfaction. Clearly it was a state with a dense population, one that depended upon trading, and with a force capability designed to protect its trading interests. It was found to have special relationships with Dacia, which explained Dacia's independence and possession of part of the territory of Lusitania, despite its small force capability. Mauretania, it would seem, also had a special relationship with Aquitania – another country with a high living standard, but with a small force capability and a low density of population. It was found also that Lusitania was a country with a weak central government, though at the same time a great deal of freedom in decision-making. It was probably looking for sources of aid. Its force capability was low, apparently due to the need to increase consumption satisfaction. This seemed to explain the reason why some of its territory was occupied by Numidia and Dacia. Numidia was clearly the dissatisfied power. It had a high force capability and a low consumption satisfaction. It was postulated that Numidia would attempt to break the almost monopolistic position Mauretania held in Dacia and generally attempt to attain revision of international structures.

All of this information was obtained from the basic capability figures given, and from the geographic position of the states. The session was instructive in the sense that it showed that an international system can develop out of the static features, and does not necessarily rely upon factors which were eliminated such as race, religion and ideologies, and other factors of which there was no mention by those taking part, such as personalities, cultures and traditions.

So much was read into the system on the basis of the given facts that it was not necessary to introduce any dynamic factor of change to initiate a simulation run. The participants were asked to enter into the next session without further instruction. The expectation was that there would immediately be negotiations for aid, alliances contracted and disputes arising, all on the basis of the given factors.

Expectations were more than satisfied: within minutes relationships developed at a rate that made the first hour hectic. Messages in writing were passed, public statements were made, agreements negotiated, governments changed, and so on.

At the next class session this first run was discussed, firstly as to its usefulness, and secondly as to reasons for decisions taken.

Students were first asked to state what, if anything, they had learned from this first run. Generally speaking they were critical of what appeared to them to be 'unrealistic' conditions: in almost every case a colleague from a foreign office was able to show that what appeared to be 'unrealistic' was, in fact, not so: what they had to learn was that it was not so. For example, a student reaction was that the pace of events did not allow time for consideration of all aspects of policy, which led to discussion about the over-loading of an administration, and resort to the use of power when it was available, just because the decision to employ power is an easy one to take when decision-making is overloaded. Another complaint was that in the simulation no one knew the policies of others, and again it was pointed out that uncertainty and lack of information is a real factor in conflict situations. One student became annoyed – quite an emotional response – both during simulation and later discussion, because another state had acted in ways which did not at the time seem reasonable. Again, it was pointed out that this is a situation decision-makers constantly face.

At the next class a second run was undertaken, and this time there was an attempt at 'role reversal', that is, students that had been great power decision-makers became small power ones, and vice versa.

On this occasion full reports were required from each actor, whereas previously a report was obtained only from each state. Each report was to be written from the point of view of the role enacted, that is external or internal decision-maker. Times of events and all details were required just as are required in a laboratory experiment. (The intention was to see whether this technique could be employed as an examination method. The results were remarkable – the good student was more clearly good than under ordinary exam conditions, and the poor one more clearly poor. Insight and understanding where they existed were clearly demonstrated. The student who had done his homework in reading widely on theory and world affairs unconsciously reflected this.)

Certain rules were agreed upon, designed to reduce the pace of events during this second run, such as making appointments before negotiation and more discussion to reflect interplay at the domestic and international level. The run ended with requests for international discussions to avoid mounting tensions and conflict situations.

Class discussion following this second run seemed to be more mature: a lot had been discovered. The idealist student, peace minded and tolerant, found himself almost at war, through no fault of his own or of others that he could easily detect. The battle to raise living standards suddenly became far more complicated than appeared at first sight – unanticipated domestic and foreign difficulties cropped up. Disarmament did not seem relevant, and international organization appeared to be far removed from the day-to-day situations that were being faced by each state.

From a teaching point of view the following observations may be of interest.

1   Simulation can be a complicated procedure requiring space and equipment: this experiment was on the simplest basis. It happened that five rooms with telephones were available, but it could have been managed in one large hall. No expenditure was involved.

2   The runs ran themselves – no supervision was required. The students themselves get some fun out of consulting and preparing a map and supplying the basic data. By this means larger numbers of students can be taught effectively with no increased staff.

3   The odd student that inevitably gets into a class and who is not greatly interested soon becomes involved in simulation – and he turns up to other classes because his interest is stimulated.

4   The absence of rules and the general simplicity of arrangements adds rather than detracts from insights gained: some experiments have been conducted in the USA where rules determine functions of decision makers and their behaviour, and one result is that all the states in the simulated world carry the stamp of the United States. Left to themselves with only the basic data given, each group develops its policies more freely, and one suspects, more realistically.

5   The writing up of the run by each actor is good experience for students that do not normally become involved in laboratory experiments.

6   Students take the subject matter out of class with them – discussion continues amongst them, leading to voluntarily organised seminar discussions.

7   The discussion classes after the simulation runs can be directed to touch upon every matter a teacher might wish to introduce into the course, and the references made to the literature and to theories relate to an experience the students have had.

We have been studying world society. We have not studied world history. This would merely instruct us on policies and practices the outcome of which has not always been that which was sought. We have tried to study world society far more fundamentally: what explains the behaviour we have learned to associate with states, why self-defeating policies, why conflict? Is the source of our problems man, the state, the inter-state system – or our inadequate understanding of each of these, and of world society generally?

Notes

1   See H. Cantril's interesting book, *The Pattern of Human Concerns* (Rutgers, 1965).
2   They are well reviewed and classified in two useful publications: F. H. Hinsley, *Power and the Pursuit of Peace* (Cambridge University Press, 1963) and K. N. Waltz, *Man, the State and War* (Columbia University Press, 1959).
3   H. Guetzkow *et al.*, *Simulation in International Relations* (Prentice-Hall, 1963).
4   R. C. North *et al.*, *Content Analysis* (Northwestern University Press, 1963).
5   C. F. Alger, 'Personal contact in intergovernmental organizations', in H. C. Kelman (ed.), *International Behaviour* (Holt, Rinehart and Winston, 1965).
6   J. W. Burton, *Conflict and Communication* (London, Macmillan, 1969; New York, Free Press, 1970).
7   J. D. Singer (ed.), *Quantitative International Politics* (Free Press, 1968).
8   See Karl W. Deutsch, *The Nerves of Government* (London, Collier-Macmillan, 1966; New York, Free Press, 1966).
9   For some further discussion of systems, see J. W. Burton, *Systems, States, Diplomacy and Rules* (Cambridge University Press, 1968); Fred Emery (ed.), *Systems Thinking* (Penguin, 1969); D. Easton, *A Systems Analysis of Political Life* (Wiley, 1965); R. Handy and P. Kurtz, *A Current Appraisal of the Behavioral Sciences* (Behavioral Research Council, 1964).
10   See M. and C. Sherif. *Interdisciplinary Relationships in the Social Sciences* (Aldine, 1969), p. 54.
11   There is an important series of African novels now available in paperback from Heinemann, and these throw light on many aspects of African political life.
12   See J. N. Rosenau (ed.), *International Politics and Foreign Policy,* revised ed. (London, Collier-Macmillan, 1969; New York, Free Press, 1969); Cantril, *Pattern of Human Concerns*; H. Eulau, *The Behavioral Persuasion in Politics* (Random House, 1963); A. and E. Etzioni (eds.), *Social Change* (Basic Books, 1964); S. M. Lipset, *Political Man* (Doubleday, 1960); Kelman (ed.), *International Behavior.*
13   P. Weiss, quoted in R. R. Grinker (ed.), *Towards a Unified Theory of Human Behavior* (Basic Books, 1956).
14   H. C. Kelman, 'Education for the concept of a global society', *Social Education,* no. 32 (1968), 661–6.
15   See, for example, N. Ginsberg (ed.), *Atlas of Economic Development* (University of Chicago Press, 1961).

16   See, in particular, *ibid.* and the *World Shorter Economic Atlas,* 3rd ed. (Oxford University Press, 1965).

17   See, for an exposition of systems relating to world society, Burton, *Systems, States.*

18   H. C. Kelman, in *Social Education,* vol. 32 (1968), no. 7.

19   From an unpublished paper by Kelman.

20   See I. L. Claude, *Power and International Relations* (Random House, 1962).

21   P. M. Blau, *Exchange and Power in Social Life* (Wiley, 1964).

22   See J. W. Burton, *International Relations: A General Theory* (Cambridge University Press, 1965), ch. 15.

23   Hinsley, *Power and the Pursuit of Peace.*

24   Claude, *Power and International Relations.*

25   Quincy Wright, *A Study of War* (Chicago University Press, 1942), II, 874.

26   Burton, *International Relations,* ch. 7.

27   H. J. Morgenthau, *Politics Among Nations,* 3rd ed. (Knopf, 1960).

28   G. S. Schwarzenberger, *Power Politics,* 3rd ed. (Stevens, 1964).

29   See R. Harrod, *International Economics* (Nisbet and Cambridge University Press, 1960), ch. II, pt 3.

30   Burton, *International Relations*; see pt v, 'Nonalignment'.

31   See D. Mitrany, *A Working Peace System* (Quadrangle Books, 1966).

32   J. A. Hobson, *Imperialism* (Allen and Unwin, 1948).

33   R. J. Monsen and M. W. Cannon, *The Makers of Public Policy* (McGraw-Hill, 1965).

34   See ch. 7 of the Charter of the United Nations, and in particular, article 51.

35   Mitrany, *A Working Peace System.*

36   In *The Theory of Social and Economic Organizations,* ed. Talcott Parsons (Free Press, 1964).

37   Lipset, *Political Man.*

38   H. C. Kelman, *A Time to Speak: Values and Politics* (Jossey-Bass Inc., 1968).

39   Blau, *Exchange and Power.*

40   See the writings of Johan Galtung in *The Journal of Peace Research,* edited at the International Peace Research Institute, Oslo.

41   G. Modelski, *A Theory of Foreign Policy* (Pall Mall, 1962).

42   R. C. Snyder, H. W. Bruck and B. Sapin (eds.), *Foreign Policy Decision-Making* (Free Press, 1962).

43   Deutsch, *Nerves of Government.*

44   Easton, *Systems Analysis of Political Life.*

45   Burton, *Conflict and Communication.*

46   See H. C. Kelman, 'Patterns of personal involvement in the national system: a social-psychological analysis of political legitimacy', in Rosenau (ed.), *International Politics.*

47   See Easton, *A Framework for Political Analysis,* and J. N. Rosenau, *Linkage Politics* (Free Press, 1969).

48   See Burton, *Systems, States.*

49   See Burton, *Conflict and Communication.*

50   See R. E. Dawson, 'Political socialisation', in J. A. Robman (ed.), *Political Science Annual 1966* (Bobbs-Merrill, 1967).

51 Waltz, *Man, the State, and War.*

52 For a report on experiments to test this hypothesis, see Burton, *Conflict and Communication.*

53 In T. R. Fox and Annette B. Fox, 'International politics', *International Encyclopedia of the Social Sciences* (Macmillan and Free Press, 1968).

54 See Burton, *Conflict and Communication.*

55 See Lewis Coser, *The Functions of Social Conflict* (Routledge and Kegan Paul, 1965), and Burton, *Systems, States.*

Select bibliography

Blau, Peter M. *Exchange and Power in Social Life*. New York: John Wiley, 1964.

Burton, John W. *International Relations: A General Theory*. Cambridge: Cambridge University Press, 1965.

Systems, States, Diplomacy and Rules. Cambridge: Cambridge University Press, 1968.

Conflict and Communication. London: Macmillan, 1969; New York: Free Press, 1970.

Claude, Inis L. *Power and International Relations*. New York: Random House, 1962.

Swords into Plowshares. 2nd ed. New York: Random House, 1963.

Deutsch, Karl W. *The Nerves of Government*. London: Collier-Macmillan, 1966; New York: Free Press, 1966.

Easton, David. *A Framework for Political Analysis*. Englewood Cliffs, N. J.: Prentice-Hall, 1965.

Hinsley, F. H. *Power and the Pursuit of Peace*. Cambridge: Cambridge University Press, 1963.

Mitrany, David. *A Working Peace System*. Chicago: Quadrangle Books, 1966.

Rosenau, James N. (ed.). *International Politics and Foreign Policy*. Revised ed. London: Collier-Macmillan, 1969; New York: Free Press, 1969.

Waltz, Kenneth N. *Man, the State and War*. New York: Columbia University Press, 1959.

Index

Africa, 48, 55, 76
  leaders in, 109, 148
  people of, 30, 5
'African Unity', 97
  Organization of, 20
aggression, 12, 34, 56, 71, 74, 79–83
Alger, C. F., 13
alliances, 85
analogies, 73
analytical, approach to international prob-
    lems, 13–14
Arabs, 124, 125, 161
arbitration, in conflicts, 151
Asia, 30, 57, 58, 79, 85
attitudes, to values, 130–33
authority, 71, 101, 111–12, 113–14
  in mediation, 153
  in states, 102–20
  theory of Weber, 112–13

bargaining, international, 13
behaviour
  explanations of, 21–2, 49, 126–7
  interest in, 10
  interpretation of, 55–8 *passim*
  maps of, 35–42
  patterns of, 5, 82–3
  political, 6
  role, 109–10
  science of, 14–18
behavioural approaches to conflict resolution,
  153
Biafra, 35, 99, 108, 111, 125, 126
billiard-ball model of world society, 28–9, 44
  validity of, 29, 32
boundaries, state and other, 20, 29, 42, 76, 80
Britain, 19, 47, 73, 85, 143, 144, 146, 158
  government of, 111
British Commonwealth, 47, 99

Central America, 142
changes
  in society, 4, 10, 58, 80, 103, 113, 137–43
    passim
  in thought, 10
China, 20, 37, 57, 83, 108, 142
  people of, 37–8, 47, 65
cobweb model of world society, 35–45
coercion, 49
  in labour relations, 92
  in settlement of conflict, 150
collective security, 42, 86–9
Common Market, 20, 97
communications
  between parties in conflict, 150–6 *passim*
  development of, 4, 29–30, 32–3, 35–6,
    42–4
  difficulties of, 72
comparative costs, theory of, 95
conciliation, in conflicts, 151
conflict, concept of, 71
  nature of, 20, 137–8, 139–49 *passim*
  resolution of, 17, 138–9, 150–63, 152–4
  sources of, 5, 33–4, 35, 44–5, 56, 82–3,
    118, 132, 133–4
  study of, 24
'content analysis', 13
'cost assessment', in conflict, 145
crisis, decisions in time of, 115
cybernetics, in study of world society, 14
Cyprus, 125, 144, 146, 155, 157, 158, 161
Czechoslovakia, 28

data, lack of, 16–17
decentralization, 33, 119
decision-making
  by state authority, 116–17
  study of, 17, 114–16, 132, 133
defensive behaviour, 56, 102, 103

177

REFERENCE